THE Beard of Avon

AMY FREED

SAMUEL FRENCH, INC.

45 West 25th Street
NEW YORK 10010
LONDON

7623 Sunset Boulevard
HOLLYWOOD 90046
TORONTO

ISBN 0 573 60258 1   Printed in U.S.A   #4882

IMPORTANT BILLING AND CREDIT REQUIREMENTS

All producers of THE BEARD OF AVON *must* give credit to the Author of the Play in all programs distributed in connection with performances of the Play and in all instances in which the title of the Play appears for purposes of advertising, publicizing or otherwise exploiting the Play and/or a production. The name of the Author *must* appear on a separate line on which no other name appears, immediately following the title, and *must* appear in size of type not less than fifty percent the size of the title type.

In addition, the following credit *must* appear in all program distributed in connection with the Work:

THE BEARD OF AVON was originally produced in New York by New York Theatre Workshop

Commissioned and first produced by South Coast Repertory

<u>*World Premiere: June 1, 2001*</u>

South Coast Repertory Theatre
Costa Mesa, California

The Beard of Avon

by
Amy Freed

Cast

William Shakspere	Douglas Weston
Old Colin/	Richard Doyle
Richard Burbage/	
Sir Francis Walsingham	
Anne Hathaway	Rene Augesen
Geoff Dunderbread/	Lynsey McCleod
Lady Lettice	
Michael Drayton/	Mark Coyan
Ensemble	
Ensemble	Jessica Stevenson
Henry Condel/	Robert Curtis Brown
Walter Fitch/	
Sir Francis Bacon	
Heminge/	Don Took
Lord Burleigh/	
Ben Jonson	
Edward De Vere	Mark Harelik
Henry Wriothesley/	Todd Lowe
Earl of Derby	
Queen Elizabeth	Nike Doukas

Directed by David Emmes

New York Premiere: October 31, 2003

New York Theatre Workshop
New York, New York

The Beard of Avon

by
Amy Freed

Cast

Minstrel/Walter Fitch/ Earl of Derby/Player	Timothy Doyle
Richard Burbage/ Lord Walsingham	James Cale
Anne Hathaway	Kate Jennings Grant
Edward De Vere	Mark Harelik
Old Colin/Lord Burleigh/ Lucy/Player	Tom Lacy
Henry Condel/ Sir Francis Bacon	Alan Mandell
William Shakspere	Tim Blake Nelson
John Heminge	David Schramm
Geoffrey Dunderbread/ Lady Lettice	Justin Schultz
Henry Wriothesley/Player	Jeff Whitty
Queen Elizabeth	Mary Louise Wilson

Directed by Doug Hughes

Scenic Design by Neil Patel
Costume Design by Catherine Zuber
Lighting Design by Michael Chybowski
Original Music and Sound Design by David Van Tieghem
Dialect Coaching by Deborah Hecht
Production Stage Management by Judith Schoenfeld
Assistant Stage Management by Neelam Vaswani

CAST OF CHARACTERS
(8 m., 2 f.)

WILLIAM SHAKSPERE: A lad of Stratford. In his early thirties, mostly. Simple, honest, very appealing fellow. Possessor of hidden gifts.

EDWARD DE VERE: 17th Earl of Oxford. In his forties. Wicked, charming, sexy, brilliant. A closet writer.

ELIZABETH: Queen of England. Between forty and sixty. A sacred monster. Wants a boyfriend.

ANNE HATHAWAY: Shakspere's wife. Lively, illiterate, promiscuous.

*HENRY WRIOTHESLEY: 20's. Young and beautiful. Third Earl of Southampton. Edward De Vere's lover. *(See pronunciation note on page 7.)*

*OLD COLIN: An ancient shepherd, and Shakspere's friend.

*JOHN HEMINGE: Manager of an acting company.

*HENRY CONDEL: His partner.

*GEOFFREY DUNDERBREAD: A boy player.

*RICHARD BURBAGE: A leading man.

*Actors in these parts also double or triple in the following roles:

Members of Elizabeth's court:
  FRANCIS BACON
  LADY LETTICE
  FRANCIS WALSINGHAM
  LORD BURLEIGH
  EARL OF DERBY

  WALTER FITCH: A playwright.

Others:
  A MINSTREL WITH BEAUTIFUL VOICE

❖❖❖ A NOTE REGARDING CAST SIZE ❖❖❖

They play has been performed with casts of ten and eleven or more. However, it's possible to perform it with an ensemble of nine in the following manner:

CASTING BREAKDOWN FOR NINE ACTORS
(7 m., 2 f.)

JOHN HEMINGE *also plays* LORD BURLEIGH

HENRY CONDEL *also plays* FRANCIS BACON and playwright WALTER FITCH. (He may also play small roles in *Taming of the Shrew* sequence, such as BAPTISTA)

HENRY WRIOTHESLEY *also plays* EARL OF DERBY

OLD COLIN *also plays* FRANCIS WALSINGHAM and RICHARD BURBAGE in the roles of ALEXANDRIO, MARCUS, MARC ANTONY and PETRUCHIO. (He may also appear in small roles in *Taming of the Shrew* such as BAPTISTA and GRUMIO)

GEOFFREY DUNDERBREAD (who acts the roles of LUDIBUNDUS, CLEOPATRA, LAVINIA and KATE) *also plays* MINSTREL WITH BEAUTIFUL VOICE and LADY LETTICE

ANNE HATHAWAY *may also play* LUCENTIO with Player's Company

WILL, DE VERE and ELIZABETH play only themselves

❖❖❖ PRONUNCIATION NOTE ❖❖❖

For the pronunciation of Wriothesley's name, I used Kokeritz' pronouncing dictionary *Shakespeare's Names* as my authority, which gave us "ROT-sley." I preferred this over the other variant suggestions I unearthed. A.L. Rowse in his biography of the Earl argues for RIS-ley, which I found less pleasing.

To Peter Franklin

ACT I

Scene 1

(Pouring rain. An old barn in Stratford. WILLIAM SHAKSPERE is sitting in a hay bale with COLIN, an aged farmhand. He has a quick face, full of sensitivity, but his hair is beginning to go. He looks like a young version of the famous Droeshout portrait.)

WILL. Oh, this rain, this rain, this RAIN! Eh, Colin?

COLIN. Eh, Will.

WILL. Look at it—pouring. Well, nothing to do about it. We can't very well DO anything with it all muck like this.

COLIN. No. You have to make hay when the sun shines.

WILL. Aye. There's wisdom in what you say. Mark it.

(Pause.)

COLIN. Aye.

(Pause.)

ANNE. *(Calls, offstage.)* William!

WILL. Like to a mouse drowning in a jughead, where all alone it sees its watry fate—so every task conspires to damp my spark without escape!

ANNE. WILLIAM!

WILL. *(Gloomily taking in the dripping eaves.)* Oh, what would-

9

n't I give to find me this very minute aboard a wide-bottomed frigate sailing the bounding Maine! What do ye say to that, Colin?

COLIN. A wide-bottomed frigate! Ooh, you're a witty man, Will Shakspere! Make no mistake! Oo hoo hoo hoo hoo!

ANNE. *(Offstage.)* WILLIAM!!

(A rat runs across the stage, a loud SNAP of the rat trap. WILL pulls dead rat in trap up from behind bale. Contemplates darkly.)

WILL.
Oh Rat! who longed for frolic
In his wild and hairy youth—
Who lunged to seize the fatal cheese
And met the bitter truth—
But no! Yet stay!
A blessed day, that ended his young life—
Oh happy snap! that freed him from
The crueler jaws of his —

(ANNE HATHAWAY enters. She is a handsome woman, older than her husband.)

ANNE. *(To us:)* Is here I find him? Playing at poetry again? Whilst I do labour all alone in care and tending—of our weedy garden!

COLIN. *(To WILL.)* —Ooh, NOW thou hast caught it!

ANNE. *(To COLIN.)* —Shut UP! *(To WILL:)* —to ME the tanning of those stinking hides that lend us small but CRUCIAL profit!

WILL. *(Overlapping.)* No one's asked you to—

ANNE. *(Overlapping.)* —must I, a WOMAN, frail and—
(Swiping at COLIN, as he attempts to crawl out.) DELICATE!—

COLIN. Aargh!

ANNE. —daily mend those fences that keep the PIG at home? And leave me stranded with all burden of your CHILD—

WILL. *My* child, I would say, but for a fretful whisper that haunteth my soul—and makes me to wonder wherefore her HAIR came to be RED!

COLIN. Hee hee hee!

ANNE. Shut up, filthy old man.

WILL. He's a good man and true as a hunk of honest bread.

COLIN. HOO HOO HOO!

ANNE. Get out, the both of you—before I swear to GOD I'll break your thinning pate across—

(Pause. COLIN's hands fly to his mouth. WILL is stricken.)

WILL. Oh Cruelty, will you say it? 'Tis true what I would fain deny—that I do lack some deal of hair. Get you gone and leave me to my friend!

ANNE. Beshrew my tongue. No sooner had my wayward words escaped the halter of my lips then I did wish me to recall them.

WILL. Have I not on sound advice spread sulfur, salts and putrid DUNG upon my ball-ed front in desperate hopes of HAIR—only to be reviled anew and called SHIT-head? The butt and jest of maids?

ANNE. Good Colin, give us leave awhile t'untie those thorny elf-knots that matrimony does delight to weave …

COLIN. I go, I go. Marry, I do but go. Aye and for a ha'penny biscuit and will I not go—

ANNE. LEAVE US!

(COLIN exits.)

WILL. You understand me not!

ANNE. —I care not! The ROOF doth ROT!

WILL. I have great … thought-like "things" within my head—

ANNE. Thou hast plucked me to the last inch of my penultimate nerve! Oh I'm so unhappy!

WILL. GOD! I'm so unhappy—

ANNE. I didn't know—
WILL. *(Overlapping.)* I didn't know—
BOTH TOGETHER. It would be like this—

(A miserable silence.)

ANNE. Was it always so dreadful? Didn't we have some good times, once, you and me?

WILL. —You was supposed to look after me for my Mum—not what you did. I was only a kid with you coming after me—dragging your spicery traps all over me, and me confused by the dangly hair, and the popping out whatnots coming at me when I'm all a'fire with God knows what. What do I know, a bubbling idiot and head of steam! Next thing I know I'm the head of an 'oushold! What shall I do? Shall I be put out as if I'd never lived?

(He puts his head in her lap.)

ANNE. Thou makst me to hear mine own tongue as sharp in mine own ears as the haggard's shriek. Good husband, be thy spirits lifted. There's Players at the Guild Hall.

WILL. I'm not in the mood.

ANNE. I hear 'tis a very low comedy.

WILL. Low comedy. Well, we might go at that.

Scene 2

(Sound of tabor and drum. The Stratford Guild Hall—The Players are in town. Everyone has come to see the play The Conquest of Alexandrio. *BURBAGE plays ALEXANDRIO, a warrior, GEOFFREY plays LUDIBUNDUS, a maiden. LUDIBUNDUS has a little bird on her finger. Two PLAYERS are playing stringed instruments.)*

LUDIBUNDUS.
Happy be this day, as our two kingdoms join—
And may our union elevate the common flock—
With those lofty arts, that with VIRTUE do conspire—
For Virtue is the use of Right Desire.

(She modestly shields her crotch. Audience applauds politely.)

ALEXANDRIO.
I shall forwith hold as dear, my Dear,
Only those delights, that do as well, instruct—
For 'tis Learning, from a woman wise as thee—
That brought my soul to sweet Philosophy.

*(MUSICIANS strum. Audience is becoming restive. BURBAGE senses
this.)*

ALEXANDRIO.
But SILENCE awhile, Sweet Music— *(Suggestive, to audience:)*
And let me WOO my love …
(Urbanely, to LUDIBUNDUS:) But soft, Ludibundus—come and
say—can'st guess what pretty Lover's trinket have I brought for thee
from fair Carthage?
LUDIBUNDUS. Oh, I beg thee—do not tease but tell!
ALEXANDRIO. It's a SAUSAGE!

(He reveals an enormous stuffed codpiece.)

LUDIBUNDUS. *(In horror, trying to make it go away.)* Nay, by
heaven, it is a cat's TURD! Fye it STYNCKS!
ALEXANDRIO. Nay, it is my PRICK! By the rood thou will
KISS it!

(Approval from ALL.)

LUDIBUNDUS. Nay and is that all that thou cans't say to Agrippina's Daughter?

ALEXANDRIO. None but this! And also THIS!

BOTH. *(Singing rousingly.)*
I stuffe my skyn so full within
Of jolly good ale and olde.
Though back and side go bare go bare
And foote and hande go colde!

(Applause and cheers.)

LUDIBUNDUS. *(Over.)*
Good folk, Our candle is at an ende, let us leave all in quiet—
And come another tyme, when we have more Ly-ett!

(Crowd clears, happy. WILL walks the empty stage, entranced. ANNE trots along behind him.)

ANNE. There. Now wasn't that something! I was moved to TEARS as well as LAUGHTER! One word—WONDERFUL! One should RUN, never walk, to see it, whilst one still haveth the CHANCE!

WILL. *(Turns on her.)* Shut UP!! WILL you!

ANNE. William!

WILL. Oh, it makes me MAD to hear you go on! Oh, these were ARTISTS—so full in fire and fearfulness that I could scarce draw mine own breath! I could give my life to live with men like these! Instead I sit in a cowshed watching my insect's life posting to its death!

(LUDIBUNDUS is working the remaining crowd.)

LUDIBUNDUS. Some beer, some beer! You, there, you whoreson with the proverb book! Is that an egge pie in your pouch—?

WILL. Excuse me? Here? Over here? If the young lady would

please to dine? We'd be really pleased. Tickled! All of you! Really!
    LUDIBUNDUS. Right!

(He goes to fetch others.)

    ANNE. Art MAD! Dine on WHAT!
    WILL. Shhhh! Wilt shame me! Come up with something!
    ANNE. Out of nothing!
    WILL. Embarrass me before my fellows?
    ANNE. These strangers?
    WILL. You kill all that gives me pleasure!
    ANNE. You provide nothing and blame me for it!
    WILL. —You take from me all heart. And do deprive me of my
necessary space!
    ANNE. Oh JUNO great goddess of domestic JUSTICE strike him
dead!

(PLAYERS have gathered to watch with interest.)

    WILL. Trouble yourself not! You have killed my soul already!
    ANNE. Invite them to our house to eat? Eat what! Porridge and
small beer!
    ACTORS. Huzzah! We're there! Good enough for us! Let's go!
    ANNE. What hast thou done.
    WILL. —There is a great spirit in me that thou seekest to sub-
due—it will rebel.

(He heads off, PLAYERS after, singing.)

    ANNE. Where goest thou? Walkst away from me! I shall not
serve them dinner, I tell you I shall not! I shall die first!

*(Scene transforms around her. Someone puts a porridge pot in her
    hands. They are now at home. The PLAYERS are at table eating,*

drinking.)

PLAYERS. *(Singing.)*
Fifty-nine bottles of ale on the wall
Fifty-nine bottles of ale—
Ye take one down ye pass it around
Fifty-eight bottles of—
> PLAYER ONE. Excellent porridge—doth any more remain?
> ANNE. Thou hast eaten everything.
> PLAYER TWO. More ale, more ale!
> PLAYERS. FIFTY-six bottles of—
> WILL. Here's ale for you, gentle friends!
> ALL. Huzzah!

(A PLAYER-MUSICIAN begins a simple old ballad. The lights dim around them as WILL crosses down to where GEOFFREY, who had played LUDIBUNDUS, is eating quietly by himself. WILL is shy, but fascinated. The others are forgotten. Except for the occasional ripple of music, they are effectively alone.)

WILL. Upon my life—a woman's face as if by nature drawn! What is thy name, fair youth?
GEOFFREY. *(Mouth full.)* Geoff Dunderbread.
WILL. All the softness and lineaments of the other sex—oh most perfect illusion!
GEOFFREY. So all do say. Well, what gets the shit beat out of you one day, makes you a star the next. Any more porridge?
WILL. Here, finish mine.
GEOFFREY. Thanks. Good man. I was SO stinking hungry. I could have eaten your stinking *cat*. I've never *been* so stinking hungry.
WILL. Thine sweet accents remind me of a girl I once loved. That girl I loved became my wife. I haven't seen her since.

(In the background a burst of song.)

PLAYER.
"Cupid ease a lovesick maid—
And bring a shepherd to her aid—
    ALL.
But what of that, but what of that!"
    ANNE. *(Impressed.)* Oooh, that's TERRIBLE! HOW does it—

(They play and hum softly for her ...)

WILL. *(Fixated on GEOFFREY.)* —Forgive my staring looks. But thou appear'st to be the prettiest maid I ever saw. But for thy one little thing—
    GEOFFREY. Meanst thou my PRICK whoreson!
    WILL. Ay thy Prick, Sirrah!
    GEOFFREY. Nay 'tis not little! I'd show thee but it would affright thee!
    WILL. Then I should show thee one wouldst affright thee more!
    WILL/GEOFFREY. HA HA HA! HA HA HA!
    WILL. Oh, manly soul wrapped in a pretty hide! Oh goodly unaccustomed laughter! Yes, I had many a good lad's revel before my WIFE drove all my friends away—
    ANNE. I'm going up to bed. I said! I'm going up to bed—

(In the background, PLAYERS serenade her to the stairs and begin to disperse. WILL takes no notice of her or others.)

    WILL. How came you to this actor's life, young Master-Best-of-Both-Worlds?
    GEOFFREY. My father whipped me every day to bend me to his stupid trade. 'Twas found out by accident I could sing. They put me in a boy's choir—and then I played before the Queen—
    WILL. The Queen?
    GEOFFREY. —who did note me well and call me Master Dunderbread. And said excellently well done.

WILL. What a life you've led! for one so young!

GEOFFREY. Had I stayed at home, I'd be a stupid ass, shit-heel retarded tinker like my stupid ass shit-heel retarded brother.

WILL. *(Searchingly:)*
"—My wife is warm and up the stairs.
"Ludibundus" is only a ... "seeming"—
How comes it that I HATE my life, and only live—
For dreaming?

GEOFFREY. *(Mildly impressed.)* Thou hast a gift for rhyme—Farmer Will!

WILL. *(Beginning to slur a little.)* No. Geoffrey, I TOO am—an actor. But one condemned forever to play in a most tragical comedy.

GEOFFREY. Nay, thou cans't not couple comedy with tragedy!

WILL. But Nature mixes both with one blind hand.

GEOFFREY. Well, it looks as if the lads are leaving—

WILL. —'Tis not the sum total of my efforts—

GEOFFREY. Look us up in London!

WILL. I've other thoughts—for poems, for plays for—

ALL. Farewell, Goodbye, Godspeed! Bless you for your provender ...

BURBAGE: GOODBYE!!

WILL. Goodbye, boys—goodbye, goodbye!

ACTOR. Give us a song, Geoffrey—

(As he sings, others pause with their belongings.)

GEOFFREY. *(A quick and bawdy ballad.)*
I asked a maid to marry me
But she said—nothing—
(A ripple of laughter and applause.)
I said I burn for love of thee
And—she said nothing—

I put my hand upon her ... knee
(More laughter, other MEN may join.)
Why she said nothing—
And then I took my liberty
And she said nothing—!

(GEOFFREY runs back up to the stair landing to where he's left his bundle. He turns. Something inexplicably magical happens. Suddenly we can see him as if he was playing to the best at court—. Whether it's the night, the attention of the players, or the flattering fascination of WILL, or some other energy in the air, GEOFFREY chooses to display another, different song—probably from his boy-choir days. He's like a bird, or a spirit. The song he sings now is old, austere, haunting, utterly unnatural. WILL stands alone, beneath, receiving it.)

GEOFFREY. *(Sings.)*
Ere "anything" was, creation was not.
And from "nothing at all," "ALL" was straight begot
And so in the mind of man, below as so above
Everything from nothing comes—
To those who love—

(GEOFFREY is gone. WILL slowly picks up a bundle and a jacket and leaves his home.)

Scene 3

(London. Backstage at the Theater. Chaos reigns. Lurid and colorful banners advertise such plays as Lusty Monks, The Bawdy Ale-wife, The Miller's Poxy Daughter, The Ur-Hamlet. *Actors rush on and off with costume pieces, weapons, bloody severed heads*

or limbs in various stages of manufacture. At the center of it all,
judging, approving, stitching, gluing, dismissing or consoling are
JOHN HEMINGE and HENRY CONDEL, the theater managers.
HEMINGE is fatherly and dyspeptic, CONDEL is acerbic. WILL
enters.)

WILL. Excuse me—be you Mister John Heminge? And you Mister Henry Condel?

CONDEL. Ay. What's thy business?

HEMINGE. His hopeful looks declare it as well as the Town Crier might.

WILL. I want—to be—an—"Actor."

HEMINGE. What arts dost thou possess?

WILL. Arts?

HEMINGE. That fitteth thee. For traffick on the stage.

WILL. I follow not your meaning.

CONDEL. No dancing, musick, song?

WILL. No! But I will learn me!

HEMINGE. Can you read?

WILL. Such question makes the very GODS to laugh. Can I read. I tell thee. HA HA HA HA HA. Can I not READ!

HEMINGE. *(Throws him a script.)* Here. Have a go at Galatea.

WILL. Pray, gentle Masters. Give me leave to study it awhile. Then, tomorrow—at this very houre, when Phaeton's chariot impales itself upon the sign of the Three Balls—

CONDEL. The present moment serves us.

WILL. —then will I show you a Galatea. A Galatea such as will set all sides to splitting! Cheeks shall CRACK with laughter, and mirth shall rise like a gaseous nymph from the bed of Jove— bowlegged with her own audacity!

CONDEL. He can't read.

WILL. Nay, I can! But slowly. I have a most pernicious deficit of my attention's ordering—

HEMINGE. What makes you think you're fitted for the stage?

You aren't very quick. You haven't any skills or training. And you haven't much in the way of hair.

WILL. What you say, Mr. Heminge, only confirms my deep assurance that theater is my home.

HEMINGE. I'm sorry.

CONDEL. Listen, my friend. What do you think there IS. To BEING. An—"actor."

WILL. Well. I don't really know.

CONDEL. It is the highest of all high callings! That which leads us to represent the spirit of Man to Men. And also to well impersonate a WOMAN in a way that FOOLS a man.

HEMINGE. At close quarters. *(Thoughtful.)* Sometimes VERY close.

CONDEL. —To illuminate the very highest and the lowest of this angelic BEAST we are. THAT is our craft.

HEMINGE. —And it is A CRAFT—!

CONDEL. Not accident that makes a Burbage a Burbage or a Kemp a Kemp, or a Heminge a Heminge! My boy, to be an Actor is: To know just how to saw the air with your hand, thus—

HEMINGE. Ay. And how to contort one's features of a piece with the sawing.

CONDEL. —how to simulate, manipulate and never fear to grandly FEIGN a passion—

HEMINGE. —'Tis the very art of—fine "indication."

CONDEL. —it is—to sink thy voice to a thrilling whisper and then all unexpectedly to SPEW! SHOUT! THUNDER!

HEMINGE. —'Tis to cover the groundlings with the spray and filth and spit of a most violent energy!

CONDEL. When Heminge here, did play the King of Goths he worked himself so into a frenzy that he forgot himself in the hot passion of his playing and ate the very properties!

WILL. *(Beside himself.)* Oh GOD! That I might have seen such playing!

HEMINGE. Ah, well, I was younger then, and full of vinegar.

CONDEL. We'll none of us ever forget it, John.

HEMINGE. Or Henry, full of invention, never out of his part—even when he goes stone dry—

CONDEL. I dry? I never dried in my life.

HEMINGE. Oh, Ay? St. Stephen's day before the QUEEN?

CONDEL. *(Winces.)* Oh, that!

WILL. Before the Queen?

HEMINGE. 'Twas during the rending of Cassandra—

CONDEL. I was playing Agammemnon—

WILL. Agammemnon!

CONDEL. Ay, and they didn't think I could do it. Nobody thought I was right—I had to LOBBY for it. I—

HEMINGE. Well, Henry's mind did of a sudden FLEE his body. There he stood struck dumb—

CONDEL. —as to a wooden block! A POST!

HEMINGE. —a paralytic thing bereft of wit—

CONDEL. Beyond all HOPE of rescue—all before my face went white! Went WHITE! I say.

HEMINGE. But then did SWEET DELIVERANCE descend—

CONDEL. Some convenient God did with golden pliers loose my tongue—

HEMINGE. —and forth from Henry issued such a Speech, so fitted to the circumstance of Agammemnon's time and hour—

CONDEL. (—'twas fear—pure FEAR did fodder the swift cannons of my invention—)

HEMINGE. —and in perfect rhyming do-DE-ca-trains he brought the act to the close with a roar of such approbation from the court as we haven't heard before or since, and the playwright told us keep it in!

CONDEL. Well he told us we could shove it up our arse, anyway!

ALL THREE. HAHAHAHAH!

WILL. Oh, Please. Mr. Heminge, Dear Mr. Condel, can't you find me anything at all?

(Pause.)

CONDEL. *(To HEMINGE.)* Well. We did just lose a—"Spear-Shaker …"

WILL. What did he play? Had he a big part?

CONDEL. Dear Boy. In the THEATER, there are no small parts.

WILL. There aren't?

HEMINGE\CONDEL. No. Oh, no.

HEMINGE. The professionals know it.

CONDEL. There are no small parts.

WILL. What's a Spear-Shaker?

HEMINGE. During the battle scenes, they come on with spears. And they—"shake"—them. Why, we don't let just anyone do it, though.

WILL. Could I BE one?

CONDEL. I don't know. You wouldn't get paid, you know.

WILL. Oh, I don't care about THAT!

(The MEN exchange a quick glance.)

HEMINGE. Can you pick up that broom and brandish it like it was a pike and a head on it—

WILL. A head! A head on a PIKE!

CONDEL. Well, don't get ahead of yourself. We'd have to see how you do, first.

WILL. *(Picks up broom, excited—)* Oh "Staff," "Pike," "Stave," oh … *(Suddenly he really looks at it—almost surprised. It's as if the object itself has a charged life that is trying to reach out to him. This may have happened to him before, but not quite like this. It's as if both violence and the memory of beauty are imprinted in the atoms of the wood. He feels it. The lyric rise of the words are almost a form of channeling—. It's eerie and wonderful.)*

— Bare, stripped, thing—

Weep thou still——for a dappled glade—

Where once thy leafing vault didst used to shade
The tender fledgling from the Summer's heat,
There thy wanton boughs did often meet
And toy with the delicate spinner's feet
Who's silken skein with dewdrops hung
Would catch the careless bounty of the Sun—

(Pause—no one quite knows what happened. SHAKSPERE slightly embarrassed—)

    HEMINGE. I think we can find something for you.
    WILL. Really? Really? Oh do you mean it? Am I a PLAYER?

(The MEN clap him on the back.)

    ALL. AHAHAHAHAH—AHAHAHAHAHAH—AHAHHAHAHAH!!

Scene 4

(An ancient manor. Sound of a lute. A large stone window ledge. A MINSTREL sits in it, along with a rook. The sky outside is bleak. We are very high up. This is the bedchamber of EDWARD DE VERE, who is reclining. His boyfriend, HENRY WRIOTHESLEY is sitting d.s., loosely wrapped in a bed sheet. He is putting the finishing touches to his long curly hair by means of a primitive curling iron, which he heats over a taper. There's also a table, covered with books and manuscripts, some of them spilling from an old trunk beneath the desk. There's a gyroscope, a skull, a thumbscrew, crystals, specimens, and other evidences of the Earl's varied and unwholesome interests.)

MINSTREL. *(Singing mournfully.)*
For all doth blossom but to die—
The ripest fruit doth fall—
Soon thy day of birth draws nigh—
And darkness covers all——
Happy day of birth to you ...
Happy day of birth to you ...
Lullay lullay lullay
... mmm ... mmm ... mmm ...

(He hums, plays lute softly—silence.)

OXFORD. How empty 'tis to be myself, today.

WRIOTHESLEY. To be Edward de Vere—Seventeenth Earl of Oxford? 'Tis a name most mighty and famously depraved.

OXFORD. Thinkst thou I glory in it? As you glory to be Henry Wriothesley? The beautiful and effeminate Third Earl of Southampton?

WRIOTHESLEY. 'Tis true, I am he. I am that girlish Earl.

OXFORD. *(Rising. He is in a restless and dangerous mood.)* Alas, Ay me, ah ... welladay. This painful exposition shows—I am not what I was. There was a time I should have, rather, died.

MINSTREL. *(Singing.)*
—Lullay, lullay, loo—

(OXFORD pushes him casually out of the window. Crosses to WRIO-THESLEY, who continues to do his hair.)

WRIOTHESLEY. Cheer up. Thy great estate is the envy of all men.

OXFORD. Call you this my Estate? This rotting castle-keep where Rooks, o'erbold with feeding on dead De Veres—perch the very rails of our bed and o'erwatch our foul love-nest? Skeletons line my filthy halls—rotting pissy rushes abound on freezing floors—the stench of ancient merriments even now assault the nose—ghastly reminder that no SERVANTS can be found who'll stay the course! *(Pause.)* And yet YOU stay, Henry. Who have much kinder circumstance at your disposal.

WRIOTHESLEY. *(Turning to him.)* I've thrown away my lot with yours. For your dark eccentricities alone on earth arouse me. 'Tis the fetid and brilliant turnings of your mind, like to the moldy veins of some rich cheese—hath lured me to this point of no return.

OXFORD. Blame not me for your outcast state! Your Mother begged me use my words to woo you to a wife—not for myself. You mis-read my poetry.

WRIOTHESLEY. "Beautiful boy, my love, my dear—"

OXFORD. I spake only in the metaphoric terms of Platonic love.

WRIOTHESLEY. —thou dost abuse the natures both of metaphor and Plato, De Vere, Dear—

OXFORD. *(Throwing himself on divan.)* Oh God oh God! How weary stale flat and unprofitable seem to me all the uses of this world. Were it not for my astonishingly PROLIFIC pen—and my secret trunk of follies, my unperform-ed DRAMAS! I should be down and out indeed, Henry. Except for them and thee, my young, young, friend.

WRIOTHESLEY. *(Crossing to him, sits.)* Methinks this unaccustomed melancholy gains sway because thy birthday doth approach.

OXFORD. Forty summers! Well, though my face be chopped and rough, at least I've kept my hair. Ironic, isn't it. At the end, all that's left to the heir of the De Vere's may well be the Hair of the de Vere's.

WRIOTHESLEY. Ah, Youth—'tis but a phantom.

OXFORD. I can no denay.

WRIOTHESLEY. Yet, though rough of chap and rucked and seamed—thy visage still attracts.

OXFORD. Think you so, think you so?

WRIOTHESLEY. And a BETTER man you are than he who in thy greener years did with his sword taste so reckless the blood of thy lessers—

OXFORD. Oh joyful boy! (—'twas me—)

WRIOTHESLEY. A WISER man than when thou didst desert thy wife—and left thy bastards wards unto the court—

OXFORD. O mad lad! (—I was.)

WRIOTHESLEY. —a more TEMPERATE man than he who— with sodomies, and buggeries, and rapes and divers pederastic flings—

OXFORD. O silly, fond, young person—GOD! THOSE WERE THE DAYS!

WRIOTHESLEY. —Did o'ersmirch the grimy name of ROME herself—with the profligation of thy weekend parties.

OXFORD. Speak ON! and twist the cords of time's tightening RACK! *(Tiny pause.)* It's been a rich life. And Death, ever Envious— longs to sack my frail citadel.

WRIOTHESLEY. Nay, 'tis but the crisis of thine middle years.

OXFORD. My sadness doth increase.

WRIOTHESLEY. Then write thy melancholy out. It's worked before.

OXFORD. 'Tis not enough to pen my works and lock them in a TRUNK! WHY must I not see my poems printed, my plays performed? Shall Genius be bottled in a jug and forever tossed into oblivion's bottomless well?

WRIOTHESLEY. —Nay, all at court do know thine wit precocious, learning rare and gift for phrase most nonpareil.

OXFORD. 'Tis true, 'tis true. But Henry. I must speak the thing I fear.

WRIOTHESLEY. Say on.

OXFORD. At times I fear me that my work lacks—warmth. To coin a word ... "Hu-man-i-ty."

WRIOTHESLEY. Say not SO !! Oh, never SO!

OXFORD. I had a secretary said it, once. I stabbed him for his impertinence, and left him in a swamp. —I am haunted still.

WRIOTHESLEY. By his angry spirit?

OXFORD. Nay. He was but a clerk. But his accusation. Lack I tenderness of feeling? I know I soar the lonely heights. But have I

Breadth? Henry? Depth?

WRIOTHESLEY. These be damp and killing humours bred of moldering playscripts locked too long in drawers. Expose them to the joyful sun of public revels and those attendant thrills which critickal appraisal doth provide!

OXFORD. No! Expose my naked name to yet more shame?

WRIOTHESLEY. Withhold not thy gift from its destination. The public sewer, where it tendeth, as a river to the sea.

OXFORD. Shall I withdraw me from the lofty requirements of my station (—hawking, whoring, dogging, and slaughter—) to scribble Plays! DRAMAS! PAGEANTS for the unwashed? It tempts me—

WRIOTHESLEY. —Give the work to The Players, and let them do it without attribution.

OXFORD. —My soul quickens—my heart lifts—! Oh, I couldn't!

WRIOTHESLEY. How much is left to go of this *Titus Andronicus*?

OXFORD. Just the third, fourth, and fifth acts. A day's work, maybe two.

WRIOTHESLEY. The power of your persuasive art will sway the world a hundred lives from now.

OXFORD. Think so?

WRIOTHESLEY. I know.

OXFORD. Enough. I am engaged.

BOTH. *(Embracing.)* HAHAHAHAH!!

Scene 5

(Sound of tabor and fife. A rehearsal at The Theater. Full company, SHAKSPERE is there, dressed as a spear-carrier. The play is Cleopatra, Queen of Nilus *by WALTER FITCH. Onstage are BURBAGE as MARK ANTONY, and GEOFFREY as CLEOPATRA.*

Two PLAYERS are serving as slaves. HEMINGE is directing.)

CLEOPATRA.
But soft—Mark Antony stay—stay awhile
Beside the gilded Serpent of the Nilus—
And say what gift hast for me—what rare love token bringst from
Balmy Italy!

ANTONY. It's a sausage!

CLEOPATRA. Nay, but it is a hyena's shite! Fye it styncks!

ANTONY. Nay, but it is my PRICK!

CLEOPATRA. Have you this to say to the Sphinxes' own
CHILD!

ANTONY. By Great Anubis himself you will KISS it!

HEMINGE. And then that's you, Shakspere. You're on.

(WILL comes forward with his spear.)

WILL.
"Good people may see in the second part what Cleopatra doth reply.
In the mean time you shall avaunt yourselves to buy oranges and
meat-pie—"

HEMINGE. I am encouraged by this, our runthrough. 'Tis not
full blown but yet it flowers, our play. It hath been more subtle on
occasion, but all will right itself by Tuesday next, I have no misgiv-
ing. *(Brightening.)* Oh, boys, we got the playwright here.

(Pause.)

ANTONY. The who?

HEMINGE. The playwright? The—author. *(COMPANY looks
blank. HEMINGE turns to a wretched, huddled figure in the corner.)*
Mr.—I'm sorry, what is it—FITCH! Anything to say to us, Mr.
Fitch—

FITCH. *(Raising a trembling finger.)* Well, yes, actually, I—

HEMINGE. *(Distracted.)* All right! Everyone—don't stray, this is a short break, this isn't a real break!

(HEMINGE goes off. SHAKSPERE goes to FITCH.)

WILL. You're the "author?"

FITCH. Author. Author.—I suppose that in some manner of SPEAKING. "By ANUBIS you will KISS IT??"

WILL. —Oh, we can hardly bear to keep the laughter in—it's my favorite line in the play.

FITCH. Idiot! It's not IN the PLAY. I didn't write it.

WILL. —You should have heard the laughs during the run-through—

FITCH. It was meant to be a tragedy! Good day.

(Exits, bumping into OXFORD, who is concealed by a hood, and WRIOTHESLEY, as they enter.)

OXFORD. I feel better already. The roar of the amphitheater is in my blood! You, with the spear—have you seen John Heminge?

WILL. He'll be back in a half a shake of a lamb's tail, Sir. We're on break.

WRIOTHESLEY. A country boy, by thy sweet accents. Can you fetch him hither for us? There's a shilling for you.

WILL. See how God provides for the actors! I haven't had twopenny for a bun all week—

OXFORD. One of John's apprentices, eh? All starvation for the distant promise of someday a tiny part?

WILL. *(Shocked.)* There ARE no tiny parts.

WRIOTHESLEY. Of course not. Well said. There's another shilling for you.

WILL. I'll get John Heminge for you. Whom shall I say wants him?

WRIOTHESLEY, Edward de—

OXFORD. O.

WILL. Mister Doe, your servant.

(WILL exits.)

WRIOTHESLEY. Thou art over-fretful of thine secrecy.

OXFORD. My guardian would cut me off. The Queen would refuse to receive me. The ghost of my raping, murdering, polygamous Father would bolt from all his friends in Hell and walk the earth in shame!

WRIOTHESLEY. Why?

OXFORD. Well, to fraternize with ACTORS—is to debase oneself.

WRIOTHESLEY. Ah.

(HEMINGE and COMPANY return, eating and talking—a babble of voices. GEOFFREY DUNDERBREAD goes off to the side still dressed as CLEOPATRA. He has a string of sausages around his neck, which serves as Cleopatra's asps and his lunch. He practices applying them to his breast from time to time and occasionally takes a bite of one.)

HEMINGE. Company—!

OXFORD. I say, Heminge—

HEMINGE. Oh, hello, your Lordship!

OXFORD. I have some little business to discuss with you—

HEMINGE. Company—work the dance, will you? Quietly, please. Tony, take them through it. What can we do for you, Sir Edward? Box seats? Taken care of. Have you met our new Leading Lady? Our Geoffrey? He's over there on the barge.

OXFORD. I didn't come for—

WRIOTHESLEY. Geoffrey you say? No. It is a miracle. It cannot be. Say you rather Mary, Lily, Jane, but never Geoffrey!

HEMINGE. Yes. That's young Geoff Dunderbread of Christ Church Boy's Choir.

WRIOTHESLEY. I'd swear to it that he were of the other sex—the one to which I'm indifferent. How strange a thing 'tis that merely knowing in the mind transforms the eye. That where, before, I was unmoved by a smooth rounding of a feminine cheek, the graceful undulation of a wig—languid crook of a manipulating finger— just that little word of "Geoffrey" works some strange magic on my senses. I think that I shall wander there.

(Crosses to CLEOPATRA.)

OXFORD. John, I have a play.

HEMINGE. YOU!

OXFORD. SHHH. I shall want you to put it on. It's very good.

HEMINGE. But when? We're fully booked—

OXFORD. What's next?

HEMINGE. Why, *Scurvy Wives*, and then we're giving a new thing by—

ACTOR. Hey LOOK where Old FITCH has HANGED himself!

ALL. HAHAHAHAH!

WILL. Wherefore do you LAUGH! Is it a great thing to see a man driven to distraction by the misuse of his work!!!

(ALL hang their heads.)

ALL. *(Quickly.)* He's right. What a shame. Poor Fitch.

HEMINGE. We may have a slot. What's it called.

OXFORD. *Titus Andronicus*. A most Bloody and Beastly Tragedy! It has wicked prevarications, heinous decapitations, multiple mutilations, lawless fornications—

HEMINGE. Ah. But where's the LOVE,—your Lordship!— Where's the LOVE?

OXFORD. Love there is! Between a wicked Queen and a wicked Moor.

HEMINGE. OH!! I like it. I quite LIKE it. Let's see—how could it go. There's the Queen. And she says: Nay, what is that bulges there, under your Moorish CLOAK—have you brought me a good flagon of Algerian wine? And HE says—

OXFORD. NO!! John. Never. Not like that! If I give it you, it shall be performed as it was set down. Not a thing changed, not a jot, not a tittle, not a scrap.

HEMINGE. RE-ally? Oh.

OXFORD. Look at the SHIT you do.

HEMINGE. The HITS I do—

OXFORD. The DRIVEL you perform.

HEMINGE. It suits the temper of the time—

OXFORD. Offer better fare and they will eat it—

HEMINGE. Better fare?

OXFORD. Do you dare greatness?

HEMINGE. Greatness. Oh. GREATness.

OXFORD. John. FORSWEAR the merely vulgar, bawdy, bloody and crude.

HEMINGE. Here's my penknife, here's my chest.

OXFORD. NAY! I offer you the vulgar, bawdy, bloody, crude, but excellent as WELL!—EARTHSHAKING, ROUSING and ETERNAL!

HEMINGE. Well, it's quite an honor. Have you thought if we're quite worthy enough?

WILL. Excuse me your Lordship. I heard what you were saying, and I just want to be in it.

OXFORD. And you shall be, hale fellow. Plain, good, gentle fellow. What's your name?

WILL. Oh, they call me honest Will Shakspere—

OXFORD. *(Aside to HEMINGE.)* Heminge, I need a Mask. A Beard. To lend me his name. A front man who can be trusted.

WILL. Discreet Will Shakespere.

OXFORD. *(Aside to HEMINGE.)* If anyone breathes that I am connected to this filthy disgusting theatre of yours, I will have them garroted. Understand me?

HEMINGE. What's not to understand?

WILL. Trustworthy-to-the-grave-Will Shakspere.

OXFORD. How about him.

HEMINGE. HIM?

WILL. Most-Damnably-Without-Hair—Will SHAKSPERE.

OXFORD. Will, wilt thou lend me thy Will for some great Will of mine?

WILL. What? I'm rather simple. True, but simple.

OXFORD. —And in doing MY will, Be MY will, for this brief sum of Time?

WILL. Come again?

OXFORD. And in MY WILL I will reward thee for thy WILL's use to ME.

SHAKESPERE. By GOD I will do it! Whatever it shall be.

OXFORD. Only this. Be thou the Stepfather of Mine Invention's Heir.

WILL. How do you mean?

OXFORD. I will WRITE. You will sign your name.

WILL. That—could be difficult. I can DO it you know, its just this old trouble with my hand—

OXFORD. Only give me your hand on it, and we will fix the trouble.

HEMINGE. Shakspere is an most odoriferous name.

WILL. Oh, thank you! It's quite old, you know. It's a derivative of Sheep's Pee, we think. My ancestors had many a sheepscote.

HEMINGE. Why doth he not be signed Shakes-speare, is that not how he is listed on the roles?

WILL. A STAGE NAME! Fancy ME with a STAGE NAME—

OXFORD. And a *nom-de-plume*, to boot.

WILL. A what?

OXFORD. But—never a word gentle Will—must thou spill.

WILL. Not I.

OXFORD. Heminge, the author hath the right to attend all rehearsals—

HEMINGE. Of course I'd welcome the input.

OXFORD. Casting—design and director approval—
HEMINGE . —an honour to be sure—
OXFORD. Where the hell is Wriothesley—*(Sees WRIO-THESLEY with boy, off.)* —oh. A designated number of house seats—
HEMINGE. Well, how many are we talking about?

(They exit.)

WILL. Wonderful wonderful, and most wonderful—and after this more wonderful still! To lend my name to such an enterprise!—To be made use of in such a fashion! Oh, Great Fate! Fortune has raised me in her ranks from foul footstool to first-class footman! There is no fathoming her means with her favorites!

Scene 6

(The Court: EARL OF DERBY, SIR FRANCIS BACON, LADY LET-TICE, LORD BURLEIGH and FRANCIS WALSINGHAM. Sound: A spinet. Everyone is intently reading a manuscripts. They are wearing glasses.)

LETTICE. *(Enflamed.)* This *Venus and Adonis*!
BACON. I liked it—
LETTICE. And so did I—
ALL. *(Together.)*
        BURLEIGH. And I!
        DERBY. And I.
        WALSINGHAM. I too!
        BACON. The best I ever read!
DERBY. Thrice oe'r I read it without stopping!
LETTICE. I too! I confess it!
BURLEIGH. It seemed the pages turned all of themselves!

BACON. —and when the lascivious Goddess says "Graze on my lips and if those hills be dry—"

ALL. "Stray LOWER!"

LETTICE. *(An outburst.)* Oh WANTON Goddess, wayward LINE and wonderful wicked writer! WHO IS—this—"Will-ee-yam Shak-es-Speare!"

ALL. Yes. Yes. Yes.

LETTICE. *(Overlapping.)* Who is he?

BACON. Is he ... well, he MUST be ... from Cambridge?

DERBY. *(Thoughtfully.)* Do you know what, all, this poem. It's strange, but, it doth—remind me of something—

ALL. *(Together.)*

    LETTICE. What?

    BACON. What?

    BURLEIGH\WALSINGHAM. What—what?

DERBY. Well, call me of wit distempered, but this TALE, you know, of this fleeing MAN, and the older, LOVE-crazed Goddess in pursuit ...

ALL. *(Thoughtfully.)* Hmmm. Ahh. *(Pause.)* OH!

LETTICE. *(Lowering her voice.)* Why doth it not savor of my Lord of Oxford and—

(Fanfare. QUEEN ELIZABETH enters. She is dressed magnificently and stiffly. She has a large collar which may somewhat restrict her peripheral vision. She carries a dangerous fan, or pair of gloves, which she occasionally cracks on something or someone, for emphasis. General genuflection.)

ALL. *(Overlapping.)*

    WALSINGHAM. THE QUEEN!

    DERBY. Elizabeth!

    LETTICE. Regina!

    BACON. Regia Virginia!

    BURLEIGH. Magnificatus Verissimus.

ALL. *(Together.)* Our QUEEN our QUEEN our QUEEN!!

ELIZABETH. At ease, Good Friends. Do not let me keep you from those sweet diversions by which you do beguile the time and tempt it from its course that leads all men and women to the grave.

(Applause.)

ALL. *(Together.)*
  BURLEIGH. Oh WELL said.
  WALSINGHAM. Well said.
  BACON\DERBY\LETTICE. Brava, Majesty.

ELIZABETH. But where is my Lord of Oxford? *(Courtiers exchange glances.)* What? De—"Vere?" ... not—"here?"

(Indulgent chuckles.)

ELIZABETH. I had thought to see him. Burleigh? Where's your wayward ward?

BURLEIGH. I have not seen him this fortnight.

ELIZABETH. Lord Walsingham?

WALSINGHAM. *(Darkly.)* His movements be unknown.

ELIZABETH. But doth he HIDE himself? One would think he doth avoid his queen!

ALL. Hahahahah!

ELIZABETH. Well then. Gentle friends all! How ist doth amuse thyself this day? What no hawking, or hounding, nor gaming nor gossiping? How ist doth pass the time 'twixt now and then?

BACON. We've started a reading group, actually.

ALL. He did. He did. He did.

LETTICE. *(Quickly.)* Bacon. It was his idea.

(Pause.)

ELIZABETH. A reading group? What Jollity the name doth

promise. What good elevation of the common wit. Why, my Lord of Oxford should know of this. It would delight him, and please his hours. SEND to him, Burleigh—

BURLEIGH. I know not to which whorehouse to send, Your Majesty.

(ELIZABETH circles to the back of a chair, which may or may not contain a courtier—she may occasionally whack it in frustrated passion.)

ELIZABETH. I do sicken without my Edward, for he doth so amuse me, that when he is not nigh, I feel the world a dull—*(Whack.)* STALE—*(Whack.)* TIRED—! *(Whack.)* Place. Is that not strange? *(COURT is very alarmed.)* Perhaps I do ... "love" ... him. *(Pause. She remembers herself.)* I do JEST, all.

ALL. HAHAHAHA!

ELIZABETH. *(Elegant, recovered.)* So tell us more of this "Reading Society."

LADY LETTICE. Just a place to come, and we read out loud, the best of the time, the worst of the time—. We all read the same thing so we can discuss it, and—

ELIZABETH. Sir Francis? Why dost thou pale and what is it hath so sudden put away?

BACON. 'Tis nothing, good my Queen.

ELIZABETH. Then let me see this nothing—

BACON. It is—we are reading a most astonishing poem. Your Majesty. 'Tis called *Venus and Adonis*.

ALL. *(Overlapping:)*

    BACON. 'Tis good.

    LETTICE. 'Tis good.

    WALSINGHAM ET AL. 'Tis really, really GOOD!

ELIZABETH. And what is the matter of it?

(Pause.)

BACON. 'Tis a ballad of the Queen of LOVE Herself. Great VENUS, as the title doth suggest.

ELIZABETH. Why—in this our day—this era, if I might be so bold, our "Elizabethan" era, that can only be myself!

ALL. Oh, no no! *(WALSINGHAM:)* I shouldn't think so!

LADY LETTICE. Oh, not SO your Majesty—

ELIZABETH. Who ELSE, Minion, should inspire such a work but I the great descendant of they that wrote the Magna Carta, Elizabeth Tudor, Virginia Suprema—Regina Dentata!! *(To ALL, quivering with pride and pleasure.)* What of this Great Venus, and her—Adonis—my Edward if you ask me—for I detect HIS very hand in this? *(Silence.)* Hath the cat got all your tongues? Well say!

(Silence.)

ELIZABETH. Is there a Lady it be dedicate to?

ALL. WRIOTHESLEY! WRIOTHESLEY! YOUNG WRIO-THESLEY!

LETTICE. —the Effeminate Earl of SouthHAMPTON.

(Pause.)

ELIZABETH. *(Absorbing this great blow, somewhere deep within her metal bosom.)* Well. Well. That way goes the game.

BACON. Oh. It sayeth—the author is one "William Shake-speare."

ALL. HaHaHaHaha!

ELIZABETH. *(Stoic.)* Lord Burleigh, tell your ungracious ward he may return to court. I will not deny his gifts. I will hear this poem of Master Shakes-peare- though I find I fear it.

(At a look from the QUEEN, LETTICE rises with the manuscript.)

LETTICE.
"Even as the sun, with purple colored face—"

BACON. Purple colored face ... that's GOOD ...

(Lights fade and we pick up OXFORD, WILL in tow, en route to Oxford's rooms. OXFORD is reciting from his same poem—uncontrollably and happily full of himself.)

OXFORD. *(Reading from a new copy.)*
"—has 'taen his last leave of the weeping morn—
Rosecheek'd Adonis hied him to the chase;
Hunting he loved, but love he laughed to scorn—
Sick-thoughted Venus—
Makes amain unto him
And likes a bold-fac'd suitor 'gins to woo him—"

Scene 7

(New scene completes building as WILL and OXFORD enter Oxford's rooms. OXFORD is in high good humor. They are carrying a short stack of the newly printed Venus and Adonis, *which OX-FORD keeps smelling.)*

OXFORD. *(Beaming.)* The booksellers can't keep 'em in the stalls. EVERYONE who is NO-one is reading me. Oooh. It's really disgusting.

WRIOTHESLEY. *(Entering, fastening his doublet.)* Thou lookst thirty-SEVEN again. Doth he not, Will?

WILL. Oh, ay.

OXFORD. Will. I've got another. Read it over, sign and take it to the printer tomorrow—he'll be expecting you.

WILL. *(Awestruck.)* Already? Why thou art as the gilded pike whose belly swells with countless bursting eggs—

WRIOTHESLEY. Ugh!

OXFORD. *(Struck.)* Nay—NAY! A pithy image—alive with horror of the breeding world ... are you sure that you're not one of us?

WILL. Pardon?

OXFORD. *(Handing WILL a manuscript.)* Never mind. Here it is—your latest.

WILL. *The Rape of Lucrece.* What is the subject? *(A pause. WRI-OTHESLEY exaggeratedly mouths* The. Rape. of. Lucrece.*)* I'm sorry. I meant —the "Theme."

OXFORD. —Innocence defiled, lust triumphant—rape, despair and death—a playful little nothing, really.

WRIOTHESLEY. Oh, now, you've horrified him.

OXFORD. Oh, no. I think I've aroused him.

WRIOTHESLEY. *(Picks up hourglass.)* Oh, Edward, look at the time! We're LATE!

WILL. *(Reading.)*
"Let him have time to tear his curled hair
Let him have time against himself to rave ...
Let him have time ..."

What in the WORLD is that repeating thing?

WRIOTHESLEY. What—fellow—wert born in a BARN! *(Catches himself.)* —Sorry.

OXFORD. Why 'tis a poetic figure. Its called *Anaphora.*

WRIOTHESLEY. Everyone knows that ...

WILL. Of course ...

OXFORD. *(Selecting a book.)* And you might read this. You'd better know SOMETHING, if you're to be in the game.

WILL. Forgive me, Lordship, for a clodpate and a fool.

OXFORD. Why, never ask pardon for thine inquiry. 'Tis a marvellous thing—when a man's hunger grows greater than his shame. *(He smiles at WRIOTHESLEY—touches him lightly. They start out.)* Oh, lower the Gate when you leave, will you?

(They exit. WILL sits down tentatively at Oxford's desk, opens book— Puttenham's The Art of English Poesy *or something like it.)*

Scene 8

(The barn in Stratford. ANNE enters, a folded packet in her hand.)

ANNE. He hath left my heart in PIECES! Lies not WITH me, lies TO me—then gone from me!—GONE without a word these many months! And now this morning comes another packet—*(Unseals packet—impressed.)* Ten shillings! I've never even SEEN ten shillings! Ooooh! Oooh! Once he loved me. I know it by all of woman's surety. Oh, damned be my woman's pride! Desperate measures for a desperate time! I'll follow him and charm him back anew!

(COLIN enters with a bowl of milk.)

COLIN. Has't seen my pussy? *(Goes behind hay bale.)* Here puss puss puss!

ANNE. A plan informs me! 'Tis desperate—ill, yet well! This night I'll steal away clad in old Colin's vile rags—for then who on all the vasty stretch of highway wouldst dare to lay finger to such a loathsome bundle! Colin!

COLIN. Harrgh?

ANNE. Sweet Colin, good Colin, gentle Colin—give me thy disgusting other outfit. The one that thou art wont to wear to church—and I will give thee a silver shilling for it.

COLIN. Hoohoohoo. I will for a shilling, No marry I will. For one such a shilling I will—

ANNE. Curb thy TONGUE!

COLIN. I go, I go.

ANNE.
And thus disguised, to London I will stray
And there my husband may discover—
That meat again as sweet—that once was cast away!

Scene 9

(Sound of tabor and drum. The Theater. A frustrating rehearsal of Titus Andronicus. *GEOFFREY as LAVINIA, bleeding stumps for arms. BURBAGE is MARCUS, and WILL holds a spear and hunting horn. OXFORD sits, somewhat traumatized, to the side while a player or two enthusiastically show him severed heads, buckets of blood they've made, etc. Others sit on sidelines, sewing, reading, stretching.)*

HEMINGE. All right, Richard. Once more from "speak gentle niece," and I think ... *(Confidentially.)* We might be MISSING something here. A different ... color, perhaps. *(OXFORD looks up in horror.)* This Lavinia IS his FAVORITE niece, of course, and this dreadful THING hath happened—her hands have been hacked OFF of course—her tongue hath been ripped OUT of course—but Uncle Marcus isn't a man without HUMOR. There's a bit of a glimmer to the man, don't you think? *(BURBAGE radiates good cheer.)* A TWINKLE in him? Find the warmth.
OXFORD. No.

(BURBAGE radiates tragic misery.)

HEMINGE. Forget what I said. Once more, then.
MARCUS.
Speak, gentle niece!
Why dost not speak to me?
(LAVINIA spits out an enormous bloody tongue.)
Alas! A crimson river of warm blood,
Like to a bubbling fountain stirred with wind,
Doth rise and fall between thy ros-ed lips—
(Beats his breast—a rising shout of anguish.) Aaaaaaa-AAAAAHHH!

WILL. *(As HUNTSMAN, sobbing.)* Gahh! GAHH GAHH!

BURBAGE. WHAT! Though upstart piece of Stage Dressing! Maks't sound upon my LINE—Hayseed! MOVE while Burbage SPEAKS! KNAVE! I KILL thee!

(BURBAGE flies at WILL.)

HEMINGE. PEACE! Richard—RICHARD! Let's break. Huntsman?

WILL. Yes?

HEMINGE. Don't pull focus. Just stand there!

WILL. Could any Huntsman look on such a spectacle unmoved?

HEMINGE. Yes, I think so.

WILL. Nay, I'll not believe it! Nor will I so betray my art to show NOT the passion of the Huntsman's heart! HOW shall I keep it IN if I so feel it!

HEMINGE. He would not MOVE!

WILL. Give me one REASON! I crave but a REASON that he may in good conscience stand stock-still as you would have me!

OXFORD. *(Looking up from his manuscript.)* The Huntsman—is—bewitched. Some strange spell rooteth him, soundless, to the ground.

HEMINGE. That's it.

WILL. Marvellous! Most Marvellous! I can PLAY that.

(HEMINGE leaves in disgust. BURBAGE starts for SHAKSPERE in a fury.)

BURBAGE. Play THIS you butchering fumbler! Nitwit! FEEL THIS you snotterweeded—halfbaked jack'o'leg!!

OXFORD. Hullo, Dick. I hear 'tis good to sit cross-legged and say your prayers backward.

(BURBAGE stops.)

BURBAGE. What say you?

OXFORD. *(Provokingly.)* What say *you?* How?—So far from thy good kidney?

BURBAGE. Am I a lion that I shall roar, or do you put me in mind of the asses' poxy fable—

OXFORD. An ass? Who's an Ass!

BURBAGE. Why, asses are everywhere, lookst well upon thy boot-top!

OXFORD. Nay, I cannot for my Leg is too high and will not Bend!

BURBAGE. *(Fondly.)* Nay, Plague upon your Lordship. I am out.

BOTH. HAHAHAHAH!

(They exchange a hearty embrace and BURBAGE exits.)

WILL. What was that!

OXFORD. Extemporaneous mother-wit. I believe he would have killed you had I not so deftly diverted him.

(OXFORD is making notes. WILL approaches him timidly)

WILL. —Well, my Lord, 'tis a part to DIE for.

OXFORD. What's that?

WILL. The Huntsman.

OXFORD. Really.

WILL. Behold, my hands. They shake with wonder and terror and pity.

OXFORD. Really?

WILL.
"A crimson river of warm blood
Like to a bubbling fountain stirred with wind"
How can'st thou think of such a thing, where I might just have said—*(Searchingly.)* "Howl. Howl. Howl."

OXFORD. Ah. Hmm.

WILL. 'Tis wonderful.

OXFORD. Yes, my boy, 'tis the extra and unnecessary artifice that is the spark and superfluity of our art.

WILL. I wonder, well. It's just a little thing—

OXFORD. What is it? Speak freely if th'art not afraid to die—

(OXFORD grabs WILL by the lapels.)

WILL. Nay—it's just this. How came'st thou so to dip thy pen in light—and write in words so bright that e'en the supris-ed sun doth dim when Oxford doth appear?

OXFORD. *(Pleased. A little surprised.)* Oh! Well said! Thou art a witty fellow. *(Releasing him.)* You know, it's true. Never has the thrill and surge of my mighty language carried me so high aloft and yet so dizzyingly deep. This *Titus Andronicus* shall make—thy—name, Shakespeare.

(They laugh.)

WILL. On what anvil turn thee thy mighty lines? How comes such GENIUS to pass!

OXFORD. Why, let me think. Oh, well, there's my many years of fine, fine, education and enforced culture at the hands of my Hated Guardian, of course ...

WILL. Ah.

OXFORD. Yes, I had all the best Masters, all great poets in their own rights.

WILL. How I *regret* me that I did not stick in school.

OXFORD. *(Overlapping him.)* —Brave Pliny and Good Lucas, Sweet Ovid, Plato, yes I had to become utterly familiar with them all.

WILL. *(Despairing.)* I have but small Latin and less Greek!

OXFORD. Why Will! 'Tis no matter for an actor.

WILL. Doth think thy marvelous art derives from thy course of study?

OXFORD. Oh, nay, nay. One must write what one hast lived, of course.

WILL. Of course!

OXFORD. My painful life hath gi'n me most expensive opportunities to taste of tragedy.

WILL. Mine TOO!

OXFORD. The murder of my Lordly Father, the treachery of my beautiful and gifted mother. Then the long exile I endured to the continent while my lover languished in the tower—

WILL. —I have seen a girl of fifteen drowned in a duck pond—

OXFORD. Ay, and thou shall speak to me of it, anon. I was captured by Pirates, you know, did I tell you?

WILL. No, but this girl, she —was floating face up and she got flowers in her hair—

OXFORD. *(Overriding him.)* What else—what else? Oh! I've fought, you know, at the front lines—

WILL. GOD!

OXFORD. —thrown myself in the thundering cannon's path for Rank doth have its Obligations.

WILL. Now, I've poached, of course. And run me like hell from those as who would have done me deep injury. 'Twas reckless, but I was a youth, tasting of adventure.

OXFORD. What more, what more. I've loved both men and women, Whores of either sex, Royalty and those of royal blood.

WILL. I was trapped into marriage by the first woman I lay with.

OXFORD. *(Throwing a thoughtful arm around WILL.)* —Yes, I've waded deep in every kind of fornication that the waste of my estate could yield. And now, like to the ancient eagle, whose beak hath, unexpected, broke with plucking on the young rabbits—dream only of some peaceful aerie where I might with only one young lamb (or maybe two at most) feed more restfully and rake the countryside no more.

WILL. I stand amazed.

OXFORD. And from all this, my friend, this tattered, checkered and wild expanse of my life—have I welded my great Art!!

(Pause.)

WILL. My Lord? I have a question burns me, kills me, leaves me no peace till it be answered.

OXFORD. What?

WILL. Do you think that I have ... "talent?"

OXFORD. Why Will! You're serious!

WILL. From the bottom of my heart.

OXFORD. Well, thou art indeed honest, and of an open and free nature. Thou art a regular Philomel. Artless and sweet.

WILL. My heart sinks.

OXFORD. Thou hast an excellent fancy, brave notions, and gentle expressions. Thou art a truehearted and goodly fellow.

WILL. Worse and worse!

OXFORD. Beware, Will Shakspere. Fly not near the flame of ART. If thou are not made of strong enough mettle she will snap thee in half—

WILL. I'm game—

OXFORD. —cut thy balls off—

WILL. I am not afraid!

OXFORD. —and throw thee back to the world with all the world spoilt for thee—

WILL. Then let it COME—! though I be charred, blasted, shamed, wrecked for it—a twitching idiot who looked into the sun—a broken man who dared to love a Goddess—too burned to fly, too sad to crawl—a sot-wit tavern dreamer—a mumbling prophet surrounded by halfwits, judged by fools, ABANDONED BY THOSE BRIGHT ANGELS THAT HE ONCE HARNESSED TO HIS WILL—

OXFORD. *(Surprised.)* That's not bad ...

WILL. It's—what—I—want!

END OF ACT ONE

ACT II

Scene 1

(London. Upstage is Will's room. It's furnished simply: an unmade bed, a table and some books. Downstage, ANNE alone. She talks to us.)

ANNE. Ooooh, LONDON! Well, life is certainly strange. 'Twould never be believed in a FICTION that my own husband might not penetrate my disguise—. Oooh, what adventures have I had! Once arrived in Colin's rags, I went to see my cousin Lucy, a bawd about town. *(A MAN dressed as LUCY enters with an assistant and an armful of clothes and a hairpiece.)* She took me in and thrilling to my device, outfitted me in her own sluttish fashion. *(Fast, festive music. Through the following, LUCY disrobes ANNE of Colin's rags, snaps her into pieces of costume appropriate for a woman of lively morals, including a corset, a hairpiece, choker and gloves.)* Such THINGS she has! That push you IN where you go OUT, and puff you OUT where you don't, actually. Paints as white as poison and rouge as red as roses! Cheek patches, corsets, chokers and gloves ... shoes that make you taller than your own dumpy self—for once in my life I'm slender! *(Transformation is now completed.)* No wonder why my husband loves the theater! I never want to go home again—and just look at this hair! *(LUCY and ASSISTANT exit with rags. ANNE looks at herself enthralled. She's gorgeous, comic and dangerous, in a kind of "Carmen" way. She tears up.)* Had I only been a man, I might have been an ... actress. *(Pause.)*

Well. Thus trimmed and decked I sought out my own love—
(Crosses to Will's room.)—and contrived to meet him just after the
matinee. (*Titus Andronicus*—now THAT be entertainment!) Well. He
knew me not as his wife, but thought me a wicked whore. He took me
to his rooms, and we've scarcely been apart for a week. I've been just
AWFUL to him. It's been WONDERFUL. Well, he himself hath
taught me cruel inconstancy, since faithful kindness prompted him to
flee.

(WILL enters with a flagon of wine.)

WILL. I hope this will thee satisfy, for three times thou has sent
me out for wine, each time complaining of the taste.

ANNE. I'll be gone.

WILL. No. Stay—. Thou art a gamesome slut, Dear Lucy—why
is't that I love thee so well?

ANNE. Because I love not thee.

WILL. *(Dragging her to the bed.)* Nay, thou liest! How could'st
thou do those things which we two do together under night's dark
coverlet—those wild and stormy expanses of uncharted filth which
mark the passing of our hours together—if thou lov'st not me?

ANNE. Why it must follow that if I lov'st thee, I could not do
such filth together with thee.

WILL. My sense follows not yours—

ANNE. For I must despise thee to use thee so, ay—marry—for
who should play such games as to—*(Producing a whip.)*—whip
thee—*(Cracks it.)*—tie thee up—*(with make-shift bondage apparatus
that hangs from bedposts.)*—call thee naughty names and romp with
thee who had carried the candle of immortal LOVE? *(He's consumed
with lust—snorts and snaps at her—she breaks away, cool.)*—But
Women's Affections do evaporate like dew at the sight of red-faced
snorting desire, and hath since the old time.

WILL. *(In despair.)* You do wound me to the quick. You laugh at me and scorn me!

ANNE. Nay I do but jest. I do never despise thee, Will.

WILL. Oh, Cruelty was ne'er so fair. And not even so FAIR—and yet I am enslaved.

ANNE. —Though at times I like thee for a good fellow, and a fine sport.

WILL. Fine SPORT! Oh, these words do sound the death knell in my ear! Wilt thou drive me mad? Inconstant woman! On Tuesday last though dids't swear thou lov'd me. I gave thee my purse—ay, and my heart with it, and then on Wednesday thou lov'st me not.

ANNE. I am a woman. We are changeable.

WILL. By troth I see no more in you than in what nature sells, being damaged, on the cheap.

ANNE. I needeth not to listen to this railing. I go, I go. Seek me no more, for I do fly thee. Where's the rest of my hair and my false breasts, too, which wearing, I came hither withal.

WILL. *(Despairing.)*
Leave thy wig, and thy false breasts leave too—
And leave me with the better part of you.
As a loathsome disease ever longs for that which makes it sicker, so doth my perverted palette incline to you, foul Leprosy that I adore!

ANNE. Ooooh! Thou sayest the nicest things. Which reminds me—when are you going to put me in one of your plays?

(OXFORD enters. ANNE, startled, retreats.)

OXFORD. Hello, hello, dear boy.—Forgive me awakening you so late—but I was flipping through the *Menaechmi of Plautus*, and bethought me it might do well adapted for the Summer Months—set in Syracusa perhaps. Oh—I didn't know you had company!

ANNE. *(Reemerging, flirts.)* I'm not company. I'm a demon.

WILL. May I present my mistress, Lucy. Lucy, this is Lord O.

OXFORD. Call me O.

ANNE. Call me Abhorred Leprosy. For my Will doth call me so.

OXFORD and ANNE. HAHAHAHA.

OXFORD. *(Aside, approving.)* A hot bitch—by'r'Laken

ANNE. *(Aside, approving.)* A gay blade—by'r'Lord—

WILL. Will you embarrass me before my friend? Will you have some wine, my lord? If my Lady hath not swilled it all?

ANNE. Nay, Will, and I had but a glass—here's a bottle of a fine Rhenish red—shall I heat it up for you Lord O?

OXFORD. Don't put yourself out.

ANNE. Nay, and Will was to it himself to put me out, your Lordship saved me from such a fate by his most portune arrival—

OXFORD. What, gentle Will—throw such a lively lady out into the cold night—

WILL. Truth and lies do alternate like bubbles in a fast disturbed stream—you'll find it best to not believe a word she says, and hope, being ne'er beguiled, converts not into disappointment.

OXFORD. So sour? Sweet Will?

ANNE. Here's a nice hot cup of wine for your lordship—and one for you, my love.

WILL. Call you me LOVE? Unsay it for you mean it not, and do malign the very NAME of love by this misuse.

ANNE. Is he not cruel to me, Lordship?

OXFORD. Ay, most cruel.

ANNE. Well, we women are such fools that we do bend to the one that strikes us. Like as to the spaniel. Who fawns on him who wields the biggest ... stick.

OXFORD. Upon my soul, Will, a most beguiling wench.

WILL. A wicked wench to wrench a wretch whose fool enough to fall into her fell hell-hole.

ANNE. Well, there's my cue.

OXFORD. —A most savage alliteration, Peaceful Will!

ANNE. I'm off home.

OXFORD. It's too late for a lady to be out alone!—Only cutpurses, murtherers!—I shall guard thee in thy walk and see thee to thy door,—lest that thou be bothered—being mistaken for a whore—

WILL. An honest mistake I'll wager ...

ANNE. Shut UP!

WILL. Leave him be! I see what thou art up to!

ANNE. I WANT him to walk me HOME!

OXFORD. A pleasure. *(To WILL.)* Will, this manuscript I leave for thy perusal. If you have any ideas—a line, a speech, a thought, a pungent turn of phrase—that sort of thing—

WILL. Oh, THANK you, Lordship. I'll take a look. By the way, I've finished most of the books you gave me—I've got Lyly, just done Euphues, Sydney, Spenser (and oh, by the way, a-DORED Catullus—)

OXFORD. Hast read that *Astrophil and Stella* I gave thee?

WILL. Aye, eagerly, and found it most— *(breaking off, to ANNE, who has been flirting with OXFORD.)* Strumpet, I forbid thee what thou knowest it is that I forbid thee.

OXFORD. So cloudy with thy lady, Sunny Will?

ANNE. Excuse us, good my Lord. If you would but walk to and fro, I shall be with you presently.

OXFORD. I go to walk to and fro.

(Withdraws.)

ANNE. *(Private, to WILL.)* Darest thou tell me what to DO? If you love something, as thou sayst thou do— *(She turns out, beatific.)* —then set it FREE and see if it return! *(Gently.)* I will return, Will. Look not so sad, sweet friend. Thou knowst me for what I am, and know I will be true to thee in my fashion.

WILL. Dost thou call me sweet and friend? Thy unaccustomed gentleness maketh me, helpless, to turn my throat up to the butcher's knife.

OXFORD. Will, I'll come to thee tomorrow. Nay, I do but walk her HOME!

(They exit together.)

WILL. Low this blow has laid me. *(Slowly.)* But why have I not the heart to hate them? And in this strain, my thoughts do ... complicate.

For if my love makes my love one with me,
And my *other* love be one with me as well,
Than by this 'rithmetic should we not—all Three—
In happy rapture find ourselves to dwell?
If SHE is me—and HE is me—then—why—
Should we not all be one ... together?

(Stunned.) What have I said? And ... how doth it scan?

(He goes to his blank-book and begins to compose.)

Scene 2

(A little later. Oxford's bedroom. ANNE is waiting for him alone in his bed, suddenly apprehensive.)

ANNE. My Lord—what says this motto, stitched into your ancient sheets—
OXFORD. *(Entering, loosely dressed.)* "Semper malefacere—delectatio animi nostri."
ANNE. And say, what does it mean?
OXFORD. "Ever to do Ill, our sole delight."

(OXFORD moves to her.)

ANNE. Perhaps I shall learn Latin. Your ring—what strange figures are those?

OXFORD. Why 'tis a scene of Classical Love—most cunning—

ANNE. Might I see it nearer?

OXFORD. Mmmm hmm.

(He takes it off and gives it to her. She pretends to study it ... slides it onto her thumb. OXFORD begins to make his moves. They disappear under a sea of writhing sheets. ANNE emerges.)

ANNE. *(Aside.)* How strange! I find I do not think upon the children. What hilarity is this! I feel so very far from Stratford—and find I do not miss it!

(She disappears again under sheet. Strange movements. OXFORD emerges.)

OXFORD. *(Aside.)* By Jupiter, I feel sorry for my friend, my gentle Will. For well I know how he burns in love for her. Can it be this is what men call a SCRUPLE? How peculiar!

(OXFORD returns to business. ANNE emerges.)

ANNE. *(Aside.)* This careless and attractive lord deprives me of all woman's reason! I came to town to woo my husband back, but now I find his image in my mind doth blur!—How odd!

OXFORD. *(Aside.)* I lose my heart for this debauchery—. Can it be a prick of what some call "conscience" that so deactivates my prick? Or is it only the return of the French disease? My dear—

ANNE. My Lord—

OXFORD. *(Getting up.)* My friend does love you as his lady—. We shall no further in this affair. "An goodly man is hard to find." Goes the adage. He hath confided to me he burns to marry you.

ANNE. What! His villainy goes farther than I thought! The idiot HATH married me and knows it not.

OXFORD. What say you?

ANNE. *(Getting up.)* He married me and left me for the stage. I, knowing men's desire for fruits which are forbid, did follow him, in this strumpetly disguise. So did I beguile him with promise of abuse. And so, like a sick charm, did I enslave him to me anew.

OXFORD. You're his WIFE? By custom, law of God? Bound to him by Contract most Holy?

ANNE. Ay.

OXFORD. By Priapus, I find my appetite revives! Honor then demands I do the job. Why, e'en now my friend doth feel the horns burst forth upon his brow and knows not why—

(He charges her, she shrieks, he picks her up and swings her onto the bed.)

Scene 3

(A little later. Shakspere's room. WILL alone.)

WILL. How my forehead aches! I cannot hate my benefactor for I love him. I cannot hate her, for I am her slave. What shall I do! My noble friend and my Fell-Hell-hole bed together, and I wish myself (in truth)—between them! *(Pause.)* I am confused! Oh, I am on FIRE! The agony! The IRONY! How ist a WHORE's Kiss provokes the lyric art an honest wife could not! I am driven to the writing-cure that Edward recommends—

"Two loves have I, one of Comfort, one of ... False hair—?"

(WILL buries his face in his hands, disgusted. OXFORD comes in,

somewhat shamefaced.)

OXFORD. Hello.
WILL. *(Stiffening.)* My Lord.
OXFORD. You are angry.
WILL. Nay.
OXFORD. Can't blame you.
WILL. I'm not.
OXFORD. Dost not thou wish to run me through the head?
WILL. And so repay your Lordship's great deserts?
OXFORD. Don't you want to fly at me and tear me all to pieces?
WILL. And thus discharge my debt for all your kindness?
OXFORD. Are you not enraged, isn't your blood boiling! Knowing I did cuckold thee—
WILL. —'tis not my place to—
OXFORD. Three times?
WILL. *(Flies at him.)* I WILL KILL THEE FOR IT AND HER TOO!
OXFORD. *(Happily.)* Good lad! To it!
WILL. Urge you me in this bloody course?
OXFORD. I'm BORED! I'm WEARY and SICK of the WORLD! I little care if I kill you or you kill me! 'Tis all one.
WILL. Nay. I cannot kill thee. For you are a sick and melancholy bastard who better needeth counsel than killing.

(Pause. A male-bonding moment.)

OXFORD\WILL. HAHAHAHAHAHAH!
WILL. *(Miserably.)* Oh. Why take her from me!! Thou likest not even GIRLS!
OXFORD. Will, I never can see any bond of love but I must break it. No happy spell but I must unmake it. I can't help it. I'm not proud of it, but there you have it.

WILL. Do you have no thought of Almighty God?

OXFORD. My most BRILLIANT criminality hath done nothing to invite his notice, and sadly I must conclude, He is as dead as my dead father.

WILL. Why 'tis ATHEISM!

OXFORD. It's all the thing 'mongst the better sort at court. What's this? *(Perching on Will's desk, he reads poem.)* "Two loves have I, one of comfort, one of—false hair—?" Meant to be about your lady?

WILL. *(Embarrassed.)* —and you, my benefactor.

OXFORD. Well, which is which?

WILL. Well, she, of course, of the false hair— *(OXFORD removes his wig—his graying hair is cropped quite short underneath. WILL slowly rises, irresistibly drawn.)* You TOO?

OXFORD. Beauty's dead fleece, making another … gay. Nothing to say?

WILL. *(Enthralled.)* Fair Counterfeit! Do you think I might—?

OXFORD. Of course. *(WILL tries on wig.)* Why 'tis better on Thee than on rucked, ruined, chapped, old ME!

(They laugh.)

WILL. *(Fondly.)* To me, my Lord, you never could be old.

OXFORD. Call me Friend, rather, sweet Will.

WILL. To me, my friend, you never could be old.

OXFORD. Nay, flatter me in my melancholy and call me "fair friend."

WILL. To me, Fair Friend, you never could be old.

(They look out, struck.)

OXFORD. Oh, wow.

WILL. What?

OXFORD. *(Slowly.)*

"To me, fair Friend. . . you never could be old.
Before ... time's brutal frost ... shall touch thy head
—I'd cut thy rosy throat and see thee dead."
    I have not writ a sonnet since my YOUTH! What think you—
    WILL. Savage. Vicious. Brutal!
    OXFORD. DAMN it.
    WILL.
"tum TUM tum TUM ... you never can be old,
for as you were when first your eye—wast beheld—"
    OXFORD. Nay. "When first your eye—I— ey'd—" HA!
    WILL. That's bold!
    OXFORD. *(Modestly.)* Well.
    WILL. Ten winters cold have from the forests shook ten summers' pride.
    OXFORD. Please. THREE year's constancy in love, maybe but never ten.
    WILL.
Three beauteous springs to yellow autumn turned—
In process of the seasons have I seen,
Three April perfumes in three hot Junes burn'd,
Since first I saw you fresh which yet are green.
    OXFORD. Now, see, that's the kind of thing that simply ESCAPES me. Let's start another. *(Thundering.)*
"Were it aught to me I bore the canopy—
With my extern the outward honoring"
    WILL. Huh?
    OXFORD. You know. Carried the canopy over the Queen.
    WILL. Ah. Of course.
    OXFORD. *(Softly.)*
"Have I not seen dwellers on form and favor
Lose all, and more—
    WILL. *(Glumly, surveying his room.)*
—by paying too much rent—"

OXFORD. Get the blank-book. We might play at a verse or two.

WILL. You mean, work TOGETHER on some POEMS? Thou knows't it is my secret pastime!

OXFORD. Thou cans't no more be public with POETRY—being low of birth, than I can with the PLAYS and so forth, being of high. I could, of course, pass them around to the usual toxic fops and inbred idiots. But I can't take them to the Publisher.

WILL. I can.

OXFORD. Good man.

WILL. Posterity's head shall reel with the questions of our authorship! But the spirit of True Poetry shall not be hid!

OXFORD. The spirit of True Poetry is Love, and therefore often pitchy. *(Pause.)* William, I have a love I cannot tell. I seem—to have a block in art. Around, my— *(Gestures vaguely towards chest.)* — you know.

WILL. Heart?

OXFORD. There is one for whom I really should like to beget some verses, except I ... find I'm having difficulty.

WILL. Who?

OXFORD. Oh, let's just call him—H.W. No, better still, W. H. I wouldn't mind your help.

(Moves closer to him. Meditatively. WILL is uneasy.)

WILL. I've ... been ... improving my use of Ornament—getting a lot more polish—

OXFORD. One can see that. By the way—wherever did you get that jerkin? It really suits you—

(Sits on bed.)

WILL. —I can finally tell a trope from a metaphor, imagine, ME who couldn't tell a ... dangling modifier—

OXFORD. Sit down, my boy.

WILL. *(Sits uneasily—OXFORD beside him.)* —from a—feminine ending—

OXFORD. I want you—.

WILL. *(Panic-stricken.)* NO! No! I'm not that WAY! *(Suddenly intrigued.)* Well—I wouldn't rule it out ENTIRELY—you're a VERY attractive man—

(He half-moves towards OXFORD.)

OXFORD. *(Distracted.)* I want you—to write me—something more private and more—simple.

WILL. Oh.

OXFORD. No tapestried chambers—no flowery form, just lines that honor what takes place ... *(Touches his chest.)* here. Do you know what I mean?

WILL. Yes.

OXFORD. Quite. Well. Enough said. *(Springs up.)* So! Where's thy Lady?

WILL. I was to ask you the same question.

OXFORD. I tossed her out when we were done and bid her go to you. Came she not back?

WILL. *(Shakes his head.)* "—If you love something set it free and see if—"

(He cannot go on.)

OXFORD. *(Jealously.)* See how you suffer! God WHY cannot I SUFFER! Oh, a fit of melancholy here or there—a murderous FRENZY or two—but nothing— *(Surveying WILL's wracked form with a kind of wonder.)* —like THAT—!

Scene 4

(Dawn. ANNE is on the road back to Stratford.)

ANNE. What have I done! My ancient weakness loses me the day! I'm just a maid who can't say "nay." But neither could I well pronounce "decease" "desist" or "halt!" So now they bond, and I'm back out on the highway! I will back to Stratford, to cool my heels and hide my shame. At least let him still burn for her, which is, of course, myself. I was to have been revealed! He was to have discovered his wife in his slut and so LOVED me. But now he will discover a slut in his wife and then KILL me. As long as he thinks me ONLY a whore, he will continue to adore! I am SICK of men's philosophies. Of this mis-fired adventure, what am I to say—!! *(She takes Oxford's ring, now on a ribbon around her neck. Looks at it, for a moment. A slow burn, then a slow smile.)* That I had a wicked and a sweet night once—that showed me what life might be, if only I had not been me.

(She exits.)

Scene 5

(Court. The Reading Group. ELIZABETH, DERBY, BURLEIGH, BACON, LADY LETTICE and OXFORD.)

DERBY.
"—For I have sworn thee fair, and thought thee bright
Who art as black as hell as dark as night!"
    ALL. Ahh!

(Pause.)

LETTICE. Marvelous!

BACON. *(Moved and somewhat surprised.)* These sonnets, both the sugared and the vitriolic, are so painful and so witty, My Lord of Oxford!

BURLEIGH. And you say they are by William "Shake-speare?" The ACTOR?

ALL. HAHAHAHAH!

OXFORD. *(Not unpleased.)* Why YES! And they were only meant for circulation 'mongst his private friends!

LETTICE. And doth one MAKE private friends at a publick-house! Oh, BRILLIANT De Vere, thou pullest not the wool over THESE eyes—'tis thee, 'tis thee!

OXFORD. Nay, I protest, I protest, I protest, and again I DO protest.

(WALSINGHAM enters—courtiers murmur.)

ALL. *(Overlapping.)*
　　DERBY. Walsingham.
　　LETTICE. There's Walsingham.
　　BACON\BURLEIGH. It's Walsingham.

(Fanfare. ELIZABETH enters holding a copy of Shakespeare's sonnets. The usual consternation, bowing and scraping.)

ALL. *(Overlapping.)*
　　DERBY. Her Majesty!
　　BURLEIGH. See how Elizabeth comes!
　　BACON. Great Elizabeth!
　　LETTICE. Untouchable!
　　DERBY. Unknowable!

BURLEIGH. Pure!

BACON. Remote!

WALSINGHAM. REGINA!

ALL. The Queen The Queen The Queen!

ELIZABETH. As thou wert, all. Oh. My Lord of Oxford has seen fit to join us.

ALL. HAHAHAHAHA!

OXFORD. Majesty—I—

ELIZABETH. *(To all, ignoring him.)* What hast been up to, this dull and creeping afternoon? Come, all, and say!

LETTICE. Oh your Majesty! We've been reading the private sonnets of William SHAKESPEARE! In edition most un-authorized—

(ALL laugh.)

ELIZABETH. I, too, have been reading them. *(They wait. She turns to OXFORD.)* And they be most excellently writ.

(OXFORD bows slightly.)

ALL. All: Yes, Yes!

LETTICE. *(Overlapping.)* —Mine own thought as well!

ELIZABETH. They show more than WIT, 'tis ... courage.

OXFORD. Really.

ELIZABETH. One—didn't know one had it in One. This sort of thing. Bravo.

ALL. Hail. Kudos. Congratulations. Our Congratulations.

ELIZABETH. To Mister "Shakespeare" of course. Pass it along.

OXFORD. I will.

ALL. *(Overlapping.)*

BACON. Yes, right.

LETTICE. Quite right.

BURLEIGH. Yes.

WALSINGHAM. Please do.

DERBY. Pass our congratulations along to Mister Shakespeare.

ELIZABETH. But this violence of feeling—of "Love." It astounds and intrigues me. Being a Virgin, of course—

ALL. Of course! Of course! Of course!

ELIZABETH. —I shall rely on you, my seasoned and promiscuous courtiers, to tell me of the truth of such verses.

ALL. *(Overlapping.)*

LETTICE. Oh, love is the worst.

DERBY. Oh, a pain! O 'tis a fever.

BURLEIGH. It is to be full of sighs, tears.

BACON. 'Tis to be as heavy as lead.

WALSINGHAM. 'Tis darkness, hell and blackness all at once.

ELIZABETH. Then why do men and women wish for such a state?

DERBY. Oh there 'tis nothing like it. It maketh the whole world full. 'Tis joy, 'tis transport, madness, to be as light as wind.

ALL. Yes. Yes. That's it, exactly.

ELIZABETH. Most intriguing. To be heavy and light. Full of hope, then cast down with despair. I wonder what it is to love like that. *(Coming forward.)* Ay me. I could wish me a man to love. But I fear I am a marble monument, and not a woman.

BURLEIGH. Oh, how can Your Majesty talk thus a way. All do love her, and would prostrate themselves in gratitude before the Goddess that so bestowed herself in such like way.

ELIZABETH. OH, ARE THERE NONE HERE BUT THEY WILL FLATTER ME?!

ALL. *(Overlapping.)*

LETTICE. Nay!

DERBY. No!

BURLEIGH. Never!

BACON. Oh, absolutely not SO your Majesty!

WALSINGHAM. Wouldn't—.

ELIZABETH. Ah, my friends, Love doth not its magic make in a hall of REEDS which each their motion take from one another! *(COURT looks ashamed of itself. A few throat-clearings.)* It seems to me that Love between Two must be akin to War. Adversaries destined to meet from the first of time—longing for the battle and for who will SLAY them!

ALL. *(Overlapping.)*

BURLEIGH. Absolutely.

DERBY. Well said.

LETTICE. Indeed.

BACON. Just so.

WALSINGHAM. Yes.

ELIZABETH. I tire, and you must take your leave. Stand not upon the order of your going. Oxford, stay. A word with you.

(ALL leave but OXFORD and WALSINGHAM.)

OXFORD. Majesty, I—

ELIZABETH. Oh never flinch at me, nor round thine eyes to the exits. It taketh not a brick wall to fall on me.

OXFORD. Your eyes are even as great in far-sightedness as they are in beauty. "Even as the pitching cormorant—"

ELIZABETH. Don't be tiresome.

OXFORD. Sorry.

ELIZABETH. I must ask you something. Shakespeare. Is he discreet?

OXFORD. I'd stake my life on it. Has your Majesty a … literary project at hand?

ELIZABETH. Hush.

OXFORD. Sir Francis asked me just this question not an hour ago.

ELIZABETH. How now! Doth he think to inflict his "Three Merry Whorsons" upon the public?

OXFORD. He mentioned something to like effect.

ELIZABETH. Rash Sir Francis! But let it be. I'm sending Walsingham to your man. And with him a most rare manuscript.

OXFORD. Hath your Majesty—a play?

ELIZABETH. *(Lays her finger on her lips.)* Not a word.

(He exits.)

Scene 6

(The Theater. WILL enters distraught, followed by HEMINGE and CONDEL in hot pursuit.)

WILL. Nay. I will not lend my name to this "*Three Merry Whoresons!*"

CONDEL. HAHAHHA. Truly thou art called witty Will!

WILL. It hath not merit. It liveth not, and I cannot see such tripe upon the stage.

CONDEL. Art mad!

HEMINGE. Art insensible of this great and secret honour being offered us?

WILL. Say rather forced upon us! I won't lend him my name— for I have read his lines—and I may tell you plainly. The man hath all the poetry of a mathematician!

HEMINGE. He IS a mathematician. And who art thou to pass judgment on lofty Sir Francis Bacon?

WILL. Am I not William Shakespeare?

CONDEL. Nay!

WILL. What!

CONDEL. Thou art Will Shakspere!—an indifferent actor, capable only of small parts, difficult to hear even from the third ROW!

WILL. Henry, I protest thou useth me with no great justice!

HEMINGE. Nay, Henry, thou art too rough and speak inadvisably. But GENTLE Will, REASONABLE Will, thy name is not thy name to give or withhold at WILL!

CONDEL. Oxford owns thy name, he can lend it where he listeth!

WILL. He will not do so if he is my FRIEND!

CONDEL. Well, he's NOT! He is an Earl. And he will throw you away when he's THROUGH with you. As long as he pays you, who CARES!

WILL. He won't be through with me. He ... NEEDS me.

HEMINGE. Oh, yes, we know ALL about it.

WILL. You do?

CONDEL. How you supply him with a JOKE or two—

WILL. A "JOKE" or two?

HEMINGE. —the odd bit of "stage business."

WILL. STAGE business—? Is that what he says?

HEMINGE. He says you're very good!

CONDEL. —a great hand with a sight-gag.

HEMINGE. A natural clown—

CONDEL. An amusing knave—

HEMINGE. A witty rogue—

CONDEL. A beguiling fool—

WILL. —Clown—Knave—Rogue!—Fool! I—who—wrote *King Richard* while HE was whoring on the Continent!

CONDEL\HEMINGE. Wrote? What? How say you? Rubbish!

CONDEL. *(Hissing.)* He GAVE you the manuscript before he left!

WILL. —"I see a ... HUNCHBACK. YOU flesh it out." That's all I got from Oxford! Oh how fate hath limed the PIT! I am who I am and none shall ever KNOW it!

CONDEL. Oh, thou makest me MAD! A swollen bladder blown

full of alien airs!

WILL. Foist not BACON on me! Or mistake not, I shall run forth and cry the guilty secret to the mob at large although my ears be shortened for it!
"Shakespeare" is not some sportive tunic for
Each slumming lord, who, bored with the getting
Of bastards, longs to write a PLAY!

(Pause.)

HEMINGE. What is that?

WILL. Unrelieved Blank verse!

HEMINGE\CONDEL. Say YOU! NO!

WILL. —YES!! Without end-stop or apology! For I BOIL! OX-FORD may be Shakespeare, or in a desperate hour maybe MAR-LOWE but never Sir Francis BACON! Besides. The day may yet come when Will SHAKSPERE may be Shakespeare!

CONDEL. *(Threatening.)* Remember. You used to hold horses by the door, my boy, and not so long ago, either!

HEMINGE. *(Threatening.)* And the best of the horse holders, he was, too, wasn't he Henry?

CONDEL. That he was, John. THEY STILL ASK FOR YOU!

HEMINGE. Think, Man, what you're doing ...

WILL. Oh this I am resolved! Not Walsingham himself could force my hand.

(LORD WALSINGHAM enters.)

HEMINGE. Lord Walsingham!

(ALL fall to the ground, prostrate.)

WALSINGHAM. You flirt with treason.

ALL. Pardon, pardon, dear Sir. 'Tis only our way, being rough speaking men of the theater—'twas Shakspere only HE that spoke—

WALSINGHAM. Never mind. Shakspere, I agree. Sir Francis is no penner of plays.

WILL. Oh, Sir. You do me honor to admit my taste.

WALSINGHAM. Too long the court hath suffered with his epic poems.

ALL. Exactly. We agree.

WALSINGHAM. Gentlemen, I have for you a most brilliant play that HER MAJESTY herself is most desirous that "Shakespeare" might write. As soon as if he started work today.

HEMINGE. Her Majesty?

CONDEL. The Virgin Queen?

WILL. Who hath writ it?

WALSINGHAM. HER MAJESTY HERSELF—doth wish to see this play performed. At court.

HEMINGE. Of course—of course—. What doth it concern?

WALSINGHAM. It touches matters most near a lady's heart. A lady of considerable spirit and vivacity. Who hath longed long for the man that may match her and o'er master her. Who might have penned it concerneth not me or thee. That She Who Commands the WAVES—SHE who RULETH over the hearts of PRINCES—The DIVINA REGINA, MAGNA MATER, CASTA DIVA herself doth wish to see it performed sufficeth us. See that thou do't shortly.

ALL. AY AY AY.

WALSINGHAM. I need not add that you shall keep my visit and this matter secret—

ALL. NO NO NO.

WALSINGHAM. —or thou shalt to a man be dragged to the Tower there to perform most authentically in thy most final tragedies!

ALL. Well said, Lord Walsingham. HOHOHO! What a good

WIT hath HE! Oh well said!

(WALSINGHAM exits.)

    CONDEL. *(Examining manuscript.)* What have we here—*The Taming of a Shrew.*
    HEMINGE. In which the most delicate and spirited Katherine is mated with her true love, the swaggart, brute Petruchio—
    CONDEL. Well, there's a part for Dick, anyway! And Geoffery shall be Katherina, his voice hath just changed—but for a Shrew is no matter.
    HEMINGE. And Shakspere as Christopher Sly the Tinker—that starts the story off—

(GEOFFREY emerges, claps a low-comedy cap on WILL's head)

    WILL. —And another thing! nothing but huntsmen, ghosts and clowns! I'm SICK to DEATH of tiny PARTS! Am I not a good PLAYER?

(No one listens to him. A musical discord. The show builds up around the protesting WILL.)

    HEMINGE. Company ON stage—thenk YEW! *(ALL out. A couple of MUSICIANS on stage to add sense of scale. Sounds of tentative musical practice underscore.)* Are all present?
    ENSEMBLE. *(Adjusting costume pieces.)* Ay. Ay. Ay.
    HEMINGE. Great thanks to all for thine hard week's work. Now nothing doth remain but to let GOOO. To PLAY! Wonderful, everyone—let's just come together shall we, everyone BREATHE—CONNECT—. A short WARM-up please—

(ACTORS immediately begin to warm up. There's a burst of simulta-

neous vocalization and arcane physical warm-ups.)

ALL.
    PLAYER ONE. I am WHOLE I am PERFECT I have every RIGHT to BE here I—
    PLAYER TWO. From the Balls of the Feet to the Tip of the Tongue—
    PLAYER THREE. Rrrrotten Rrrichard Rrrotten Rrrichard—
    PLAYER FOUR. Woo Wooo Woo Wee Waw Wee—
    PLAYER FIVE. Fourteen Frigging Earls Frighted Philip's Frigate—
    PLAYER SIX. Woozle cock woozle cock woozle cock—
(... and so forth.)

HEMINGE. *(Breaking in quickly.)* That's enough! So everyone mark through any trouble–spots—

(Ten seconds of rehearsal pandemonium as follows:)

ALL. *(At once:)*
    ACTOR: "CURTIS." Let's h'at Good Grumio—
    ACTOR: "GRUMIO." Lend thine ear—
    ACTOR: "CURTIS." Here—
    ACTOR: "GRUMIO." *(Hitting CURTIS.)* There—
    ACTOR: "CURTIS." No. Wait. Aren't I supposed to duck.

(Meanwhile:)

PETRUCHIO. *(To HEMINGE, while working over KATE, played by GEOFFREY.)* Look—I take her like this and then I PUNCH her, one—and a two—one and a TWO—and then, I SWING her—

(—and WILL is pursuing HEMINGE. They're momentarily in the

clear.)

WILL. *(Over the babble.)* —but what HAPPENS to Sly the TINKER—he hath not a THROUGH line—I don't underSTAND—
HEMINGE. Will, I cannot hear thy problems at this moment—whatever you did last time—do it AGAIN!
WILL. Call you this DIRECTION!

(A fanfare. ALL genuflect and scurry to places as ELIZABETH enters, with OXFORD in tow. She greets the house and sits in Royal Box, up among real audience members. The Audience has arrived.)

ELIZABETH. My heart, my heart. I haven't felt like this since the Spanish Armada.

(Hautboy or trumpet flourish. DERBY arrives in audience, late, with a gigantic bon-bon that crackles noisily, causing ELIZABETH to shoot him a most terrible look.)

WILL. *(Playing to all, in the round. Music under.)* GOOD LORDS and LADIES. A poor, drunken tinker, taken in his cups is gulled by a mighty Nobleman—to think himself a great LORD! Now, as you shall see, I, Christopher Sly, hath awakened—in a chamber hung with silks! Play me this fine play, I tell thee! *(Uncontrollable aside, to Heminge, who's playing Baptista)* I don't understand why I'm even in the PLAY!
ELIZABETH. *(Stands up, excited.)* Nay, that's not next!
OXFORD. What?
ELIZABETH. Shh!

(Enter PETRUCHIO\BURBAGE, enter KATE\GEOFFREY, opposite sides of stage. ENSEMBLE rings them.)

PETRUCHIO. Good morrow, Kate, for that's your name I hear.

KATE. Well have you heard, but something hard of hearing. They call me Katherine that do talk of me.

ELIZABETH. *(Laughs hard and alone.)* Ay me, I fear to split my stays.

PETRUCHIO. You lie in faith, for you are called plain Kate and Bonny Kate and sometimes Kate the Curst—

ALL. HAHAHAHAH

ELIZABETH. Ay me—

WILL. *(As Sly.)* Another pint of smallest ALE!

ELIZABETH. *(Enraged.)* What doth the idiot? He hath not an-other line there!

OXFORD. How say you?

ELIZABETH. Nay, I spoke of nothing. Hush! Petruchio is to TAKE her now. You shall see!

(Now the company suggests the plot of Shrew *in sixty seconds of brilliantly inventive dumbshow. Music and picture hold at moments as actors revolve around a painted drop—allowing ELIZA-BETH's outbursts to top. See the production notes on page 00 for detailed story-board images.*
Music. Action. PETRUCHIO kisses KATE violently.)

ELIZABETH. *(Aroused.)* NOW she shall come to know her keeper's call!

(Music. More action. KATE weeps.)

ELIZABETH. *(Deeply moved.)* Left alone at the altar, oh poor girl!

(Music. Action. PETRUCHIO swings KATE up in his arms.)

ELIZABETH. *(Enthralled.)* SEE how he snatches her away from all the guests!

(Music. Action. The starving KATE is taunted.)

ELIZABETH. *(Thrilled.)* Cut down to SIZE! How like you THAT, my Girl!

(Music. KATE and PETRUCHIO join hands)

ELIZABETH. *(Ecstatic.)* Ay me! What a story! How will it end!

(There is a little trill of happy resolve music. COMPANY restores to real time. WILL, in Tinker's nightgown and cap, holding Sly's Ale-Cup is becoming increasingly upset about the tone of this odd and violent play.)

PETRUCHIO. Lord how bright and goodly shines the moon!
KATE. The moon! The sun—it is not moonlight now!
PETRUCHIO. I say it ist the moon that shines so bright! Take THAT! *(Cuffs her.)*
PLAYERS. *(Shocked.)* Ooohhh!
ELIZABETH. *(Excited, loudly.)* YES!
KATE. I know it is the sun that shines so bright—
PETRUCHIO. *(Beating her savagely.)*
Now by my mother's son and that's myself,
It shall be moon, or star, or what I list—

(Audience shocked. ELIZABETH delighted. PETRUCHIO pushes KATE down and rides her like a donkey.)

KATE. Ay me! Collared like a spaniel and made to crawl on all fours!
PETRUCHIO. *(Spanking her.)* Evermore cross'd and cross'd

nothing but cross'd!
        ELIZABETH. *(Rapturous.)* Do it again! She LIKES it!!
        PETRUCHIO. That's my girl. Come KISS ME KATE!

(He kisses her violently, then shoves her downstage. ELIZABETH in
        an erotic haze. PETRUCHIO pulls KATE up to standing.)

        PETRUCHIO. Katherine, I charge thee. Tell these headstrong
women what duty they do owe their husbands?

(All applaud approvingly. KATE is down front, secretly wrapping her
        hand for a real fight.)

        KATE. Well, I just don't know. *(Pause.)* Let's FIGHT!!!

(KATE and PETRUCHIO go at it again, this time for real. Play is
        disintegrating. COMPANY is placing bets on combatants, etc.
        During a momentary stranglehold—)

        ELIZABETH. *(To OXFORD, distraught.)* I couldn't think of
anything else.
        OXFORD. Ah.
        ELIZABETH. Something about the ending doesn't quite WORK.
        KATE AND PETRUCHIO. *(Back at it.)* Take THAT and THAT
and THAT and THAT!

(WILL can't stand it anymore.)

        WILL. *(Separating them. To KATE:)*
Though I am but a drunken tinker, yet I am provokst to say:
Fie fie unknit that threatening unkind brow!
        PLAYERS. *(ALL at once.)*
                HEMINGE. Nay! What?

CONDEL. That's not—

OTHERS. Is that supposed—What's going on—

WILL.

—and dart not scornful glances from those eyes

To wound thy governor, thy lord thy king—

PLAYERS. What? What? What? Is SLY the TINKER—he's not in this—

WILL. *(To KATE:)*

It blots thy beauty as frosts do bite the meads—confounds thy fame as whirlwinds shake fair buds—

KATE. *(A snarling aside.)* Shut UP—you!

ELIZABETH. *(Standing up.)* WHO IS THAT!

OXFORD. "Shakespeare?"—his PLAY?

ELIZABETH. Oh. Right.

(OXFORD pulls her down into her seat.)

WILL. *(Improvising with passion and tenderness.)* A woman moved is like a fountain troubled ... muddy, ill-seeming, thick, bereft of beauty, and while it is so, none so dry or thirsty will deign to sip or touch one drop of it.

ELIZABETH. *(Simply.)* Kill him.

OXFORD. *(Amused.)* Why? It's good.

(WILL takes off his fool's cap. To KATE, who is standing, slack-jawed and astonished:)

WILL.

Thy husband is thy lord, thy life, thy keeper

One who cares for thee

And for thy maintenance commits his body

To painful labor both by sea and land

To watch the night in storms, the day in cold,

Whilst thou liest warm at home,
Secure and safe
And craves no other tribute at thy hands
But love, fair looks and true obedience.
Too little payment for so great a debt.

    ELIZABETH. *(Deeply touched. To OXFORD, indicating WILL:)*
Why, such duty as the subject owes the Prince ... *(Her hand brushes
OXFORD's sleeve.)* —such a WOMAN oweth to her ... husband—

    OXFORD. *(Alarmed.)* But you, though Woman, are also Prince,
and can oweth duty to none. Great Virgin Majesty.

    ELIZABETH.
Yes, yes, yes and so forth! *(She's up. To audience:)*
OH, GO GET IT! YOU WOMEN THOSE WHO CAN!
And thank your STARS that YOU are not as I!

    (On "I" she beats her metallic bodice.) Ow! *(Recovers. Inspiration finds her.)* So—
"Vail your stomachs for it is no boot
And place your hand beneath your master's foot—
Yes! YOU! YOU!

    *(KATE falls startled to the ground and surrenders to
PETRUCHIO.)*
In token of which duty if he please—
My hand. is. ready—
May it do him ease—"

*(She extends her hand searchingly into the great emptiness of the air.
    A burst of applause from ENSEMBLE for the QUEEN's impromptu performance.)*

    ALL. Brava Virgin Queen, Eternal Virgin! Huzzah for our
Magna Virginia!

(ELIZABETH blinks back tears and transport.)

ELIZABETH. 'Tis a most gratifying ... fantasy. *(Her moment. Applause and music as ALL exit away but ELIZABETH and WILL, HEMINGE and CONDEL. ELIZABETH crosses down to WILL.)* Mister Shakespeare—

WILL. *(Bowing deeply, excited, expecting, maybe, to be knighted.)* Your Majesty—

ELIZABETH. —thou art in water most enormously hot!

WILL. Untouchable Goddess, how have I offended?

ELIZABETH. How darst thou alter by thine own actor's whim a work of divine transcription?

WILL. Great Majesty, in all the dimness of mine own humility, it seemed to me the ending needeth—work!

ELIZABETH. How now! Assaulteth me with dramaturgy? Thou Upstart CROW!

WILL. Nay!

ELIZABETH. Where hast thou gathered all thy goodly wit? From which university? Pray? Answer!

WILL. I have taken pains to educate *myself*, Divine Majesty.

ELIZABETH. That doth proclaim itself. Perhaps in the TOWER you shalt find time for those further studies thou dost evidently still require.

WILL. Oh, send me not to prison—sweet Highness!

CONDEL and HEMINGE. Oh, please, Mercy, good Majesty—no more shall actor's ad-lib issue from this our stage—

WILL. Strike me dead, for offending, I did not mean it.

ELIZABETH. Well, enough, all. My great success today inclines me to mercy.

ALL. Oh, THANK you, Merciful Majesty.

ELIZABETH. But I do henceforth command that the part of Sly the Tinker be cut most brutally short. Farewell, Good Players.

ALL. Farewell, farewell, Congratulations on thy Great Opening. Shall run a thousand performances (etc.).

ELIZABETH. Watch thy step, Shakespeare, that thou shalt not

OVER-step. Forget not that thou are in disgrace till further notice.

(She exits. Pause.)

    HEMINGE. I thought that that went swimmingly well!
    CONDEL. Quite.
    HEMINGE. Be not downcast, Will.
    WILL. Disgrace. Disgrace!
    MEN. Nay, think not on it. 'Tis a thing of no importance. Nay, whatever worketh.

(They exit.)

    WILL. Fortune eludes me, the times collude. I see too late—and what I see I HATE.—My name's become a—BRAND!!

(OXFORD enters.)

    OXFORD. Good morrow, Will! Congratulations on fine work as Sly the Tinker!
    WILL. My lord is in a merry mood—
    OXFORD. You know that *Timon of Athens* I started yesterday?
    WILL. Yes—
    OXFORD. I finished it! Except, of course, any changes you care to make. Timon NEEDS something. Give him a speech, will you?
    WILL. *(Anguished, to himself:)* —Black-white, foul-fair, wrong-right, base-noble—HAH you GODS why this?
    OXFORD. Yes. Terrific! Along those lines.
    WILL. How liketh the court my poems?
    OXFORD. Well, they can't believe that I, Bloody De Vere, can write in such a sugared and gentle vein. I'm a great hit.
    WILL. *(Quietly.)* Suspect they that ... another ... has a hand?
    OXFORD. Of course not. They think that you are really me. But

for decency's sake, they speak as if you were really you. That wrote them.

WILL. And if they thought that I were I?

OXFORD. Well. They wouldn't dare approve them, then, of course. Coming from a Player. You know what people are.

(SIR FRANCIS BACON enters. He has a strange protuberance under his cloak.)

OXFORD. Well, hello there, Sir Francis!

BACON. Ah. Hullo, De Vere. I was looking for—the lost and found. Perhaps this mild looking fellow can show me to it. What is thy name, Sirrah?

OXFORD. Thou needst not dissemble thy purpose, Bacon. That bulging manuscript in thy cloak proclaims it as loud as thou can'st deny—or art thou just glad to see me—

MEN. HAHAHAHAH

(They slap each other on the back.)

OXFORD. Thou hast caught the dread contagion of poetry—and our Mr. Shakespeare here the only physic in the kingdom.

BACON. You're Shakespeare?

WILL. Yes, my Lord!

BACON. I'm here for a ... friend, actually. He hath a manuscript for a masque—it's not done, entirely. It's wonderful. Really quite wonderful. Methinks it may play a trifle long—Ist six hours—?

(Enter several more heavily cloaked, hooded and masked figures, followed by more and more and more! Rising babble of excited greetings.)

OXFORD. *(Over.)* Why my Lord of Essex! and Lady Lettice too—why 'tis Florio! I know him by his shoes! Derby! Raleigh! How was Bermuda! Kit! How doth Spain?

SIR FRANCIS. Welcome brother MASON! I salute thee most secretively!

(Hooded MAN and BACON perform arcane handgrip-ritual.)

WILL. *(Alarmed.)* Lords, Ladies, Masons, and Lone Jesuit! Give me audience! It cannot be possible that all of you seek Will Shake-Speare! There cannot be so much Art!

(They brandish their manuscripts—and advance on him.)

VOICES. AY AY AY. I've got a little—it's about a—it runs a bit long—I just finished it—it needs work—

DERBY. There's a confirmed bachelor—this is a comedy—who—

WALSINGHAM. It takes place in Venice where—

LADY LETTICE. An Old King is giving away his Kingdom and—

BACON. Hairpox, a happy whoreson, meets Kitty Custance, a most jolly bawd—'Tis the one from which I read the first act during Shrovetide!

(ALL gasp, horrified.)

OXFORD. Well, good William Shakespeare—it seems the times have found thee out and thou shalt have a most prolific and unnatural year!

WILL. Year? Decade rather or say two for no man could write so many plays at once—why, who would believe it! We would be at the performing of these plays until 1611 at least!

DERBY. I cannot wait. I must see my play upon the boards!

LADY LETTICE. And so must I!

BACON. I was the first to ere arrive!

WILL. Hath not my Master Heminge a say in what performeth when?

ALL. NO!!!

OXFORD. Why we must all draw lots. There is no other way. And so we shall here create the unreliable chronology of this our "Shakespearean" canon—and flaming missive to the future time—.

ALL. 'Tis well, 'tis well. The LOT the LOT!

SIR FRANCIS. I, anon, shall conduct the drawing and post the list at court.

OXFORD. And thus shall we so pace our work to that of our supposed man, our stalking-horse, our WILL—!!

ALL. Our Shakespeare! Honest Will! Our Dumb Man! Simple Will! Our Beard!

OXFORD. One matter more. One play alone to all, but ten to me!

ALL. Why WHY YOU!

OXFORD. Because I have so many more plays in me that seethe and prick upon the stony shores of my beleaguered brain—as cannot be contained. And beside—this our sweet device—*(He puts his arm around WILL.)* was hit upon by me. I share him with you, but on one condition. This I shall always be—more of SHAKESPEARE than any of thee. Leave thee then thy manuscripts in yonder Incoming Bucket. And make your diverse ways before this our meeting is discovered. *(They do.)* Well, good Will, thou hast thy work cut out.

WILL. My lord—a question I pray you. If all at court now know that I am a stalking horse, a blind, a BEARD—

OXFORD. Ay, and do greatly LOVE thee for it—

WILL. —then WHOM do we conspire to confound?

(Pause.)

OXFORD. *(Momentarily stumped.)* Why, I must revolve me upon this question. Farewell. Oh—and you'll take a look at *Timon,* won't you?

WILL. Tell them.

OXFORD. What?

WILL. At court—! The poems, at least.—TELL them that I am "I"—

OXFORD. Listen. What does it MATTER who wrote them—they're OUT there—for all time. *Someone* wrote them. Thee, me, we, whoever. 'Tis all one. It's really about the work. Don't you think? Bury my name where my body lies, simplicity, anonymity—oblivion, GOD how I crave it!

WILL. Of COURSE you do! You're already famous!

OXFORD. *(Irritable.)* Look, what are you complaining about. You're set for LIFE aren't you, you bought the NEW place, didn't you— *(Puts his arm around WILL—conspiratorially:)* Between ourselves, I've really come to value your contributions.

WILL. Contributions?

OXFORD. You've a knack. I've never denied it.

WILL. A knack?

OXFORD. —A speech here, soliloquy there—some accidental insight into the soul of the common man—

WILL. Accidental!

OXFORD. —or a KING for that matter—I've wondered how you do it, I confess—you lucky natural, you devil, you SAVANT you—How DID you come up with Juliet? All I had was Mercutio.

WILL. You're claiming it all, aren't you. Sir Edward—Bloody De Vere, now Honeyed De Vere, and no one knows why. Well, I QUIT!

OXFORD. Dare you renounce me! What did you expect?

WILL. I thought at least you might sort of raise an EYEbrow when my name came up ...

OXFORD. Do what?

WILL. —create some mystery, some confusion—

OXFORD. You're joking—

WILL. —a sort of cloudy authorship ISSUE, maybe.

OXFORD. You mean let them suspect that I'm tag-teaming with a low-down small-time bit-player?

WILL. What did you say?

OXFORD. Forget it. You can't really believe anyone's going to hang a laurel wreath on YOU do you? A thing lofty, that is—Myself, may stoop. SLUMMING is a sign of LIFE! But let you come up from Nowhere—with some freakish GIFT! Without precedent! Imagine a humble kitchen garden.

WILL. My Lord has never SEEN a kitchen garden.

OXFORD. Should the root vegetable displace the rose, disorder would run rampant!

WILL. Your allegory is drawn all of rhetoric, nothing of nature.

OXFORD. *(Grabs him by jerkin.)* Correct my—ALLEGORY! Thou FELLOW! KNAVE! FOOL! Why? What's wrong with it.

WILL. Correct it thyself. If thou cans't. Oh, Lonely! I shall wander the face of the earth!

OXFORD. But Will! I am your PATRON! We have work!

WILL. I shall have lost years!

OXFORD. Your friend!

WILL. I am NO man, and have no friend. No home, no fixed address—I go I go to beg my fortune of the kinder wild beasts!—I know not where I care not where I go I go—

OXFORD. Your Benefactor!

WILL. I care not! I am leaving the theater!!

(Thunderclap—he takes his cloak and exits in a crash of lightening.)

Scene 8

*(A storm on a Heath near Stratford. WILL enters. He is drunk. A bun-
    dled wretched hooded SERVANT is with him. WILL staggers
    down to the lip of the stage.)*

WILL. Blow winds and crack your cheeks! Mountains fart yourselves! SEA puke! and OCEANS vomit yourselves sick upon the
shore! Fire unsheathe thy pizzle and piss flames upon the wondering
crowds beneath!

COLIN. Hoo hoo hoo. Please Matr Will, Colin's a'cold. Come
inside now—come in to thy wife !!

WILL. Never! I abjure all roof, all hearth, all comfort! I shall
go—into the barn. Colin—come.

COLIN. Oh hoo hoo hoo!

(Thunder clap. WILL staggers into the barn, COLIN following.)

Scene 9

*(The Barn. Some days later. ANNE, WILL and COLIN. A picnic.
    Sounds of chickens, songbirds and happiness.)*

ANNE.
Here lies the bones of old Doc Burns—
    WILL.
Whose soul on Satan's fire-pit turns—
    COLIN. *(Beating on the ground.)* Hoo Hoo Hoo!! Another, an-
other!
    ANNE.
When home to heaven Whately goes—

WILL.
The devil nippeth at her toes.
    COLIN. HEE HEE HEE—Have at it!
    WILL.
Now I lay me down to sleep—
And pray the Lord to sell my Sheep
But it you cannot sell for ten—
Please bring me back to life again!
    ANNE. Will.
    WILL. Anne.
    ANNE. I'm sorry for all.
    WILL. Nay, I'm sorry.

(They lean in for a kiss. COLIN farts.)

    ANNE. Leave us awhile, sweet Colin, to those enraptured musings that amorous absence hath so long delayed—
    COLIN. HOO HEE HEE HOO!
    ANNE. GO!
    COLIN. I go, anon, I go.

(COLIN exits.)

    ANNE. Dids't thou—whilst you were away—not that I'd blame you ...
    WILL. Ask not. Dids't thou ... Not that I'd blame you.
    ANNE. Ask not.
    WILL. Why not?
    ANNE. Thou bid'st ME ask not.
    WILL. Well, 'tis different for women.
    ANNE. Why.
    WILL. All do know why. It just IS, that's all.
    ANNE. Oh, goodly answer.

WILL. Dost tart thy tongue at me that late did vow nothing but honey?

ANNE. Nay, forgive me, sweet.

WILL. Of course, my love. How was it that I could not see, in all the betrayals of this world, a good wife who waited for me through my folly?—Why Sweet, why doth thy cheek to pale? Where flee thy former roses?

ANNE. It's nothing.

WILL. I shall never leave thee again. Blessed Saint whom I do not deserve! *(Enter HEMINGE and CONDEL.)* You!

HEMINGE. Afternoon. We happened to be in town—

ANNE. You!

WILL. Good Wife, fetch us some small beer.

ANNE. I go. *(Passing them.)* —You—are not welcome here.

CONDEL. Charming woman.

HEMINGE. You look well! Doesn't he look well?

CONDEL. Certainly he doth.

HEMINGE. How goes it?

WILL. Oh, very well. My wife has brought me twins in my two years absence.

CONDEL\HEMINGE. Oh, congratulations. Congratulations.

CONDEL. We'll get right to the point. Things aren't going well back at the playhouse. Awful.

HEMINGE. Terrible.

CONDEL. Couldn't be worse.

HEMINGE. These noble plays are unperformable! And I speaketh as one who hath produced *Scurvy Wives*!

WILL. Why come you all this way to tell this to ME? A self-inflated pig's bladder?

CONDEL. Many things were spoke in haste that were regretted later.

WILL. Ah. *(Pause.)* Really terrible, are they?

HEMINGE. Beyond all believing. One for example, this *Lear*

and his Daughters—by Lady Lettice—

CONDEL. Ghastly!

HEMINGE. Nothing but the reading of a WILL all the way to the FINIS—what MEANS this lady—"my pewter spoon—china-soup dish—my hundred pair of shoes, and on and on and on—a hundred pages!

CONDEL. She said all people of quality 'twould be interested in the extent of the Royal King's possessions.

HEMINGE. We're done if we present it.

(HEMINGE sits heavily by WILL.)

WILL. A pity.

CONDEL. And My Lord of Derby's play!

WILL. Oh?

HEMINGE. *Any Way You Want It.* A "romp!" Two lords ride into the forest, of a Sunday, and there do murder every living thing that moves within its leafy confines. This be the sum and total of its action.

CONDEL. Further he proposeth to incorporate a bear and BAIT it.

HEMINGE. Further, both Lords are named Jock. Because, my lord sayeth, it is his favorite name. *(Pause.)* There is a part for you, if you're interested.

WILL. Ah! Which? A clown, a bumpkin, or a ghost?

HEMINGE. Old Adam. The torturer.

WILL. A Torturer! *(He laughs, it's the relaxed laugh of a free man.)* I cannot play a torturer. I love all things living. Why even when I was a lad, when the butchering began in November ... I would hie me to the forest of Arden—and hide me there.

(WILL crosses away from them. The MEN watch him, aware of a change in him.)

CONDEL. Why, Will. I thought thou wast a poacher of deer.

WILL. *(Thoughtfully.)* ... I was so branded, but truly, I could not kill me one. It irked me so that the poor dappled fools being native burghers in their own city should in their own confines with forked heads have their round haunches gored ...

HEMINGE. *(To CONDEL.)* See that's exactly what it needs!

WILL. *(Lost in the sweetness of the memory.)* —Oh, sweet Arden—. You know, really, it was there—in the gentle and flowing breast of nature, that I found my tongue. In trees. My books in running brooks and good in everything.

CONDEL. —a gentler thought was never spoke—

HEMINGE. *(Outburst.)* Will! Come back with us. And bend your thought upon this most vile comedy.

WILL. Apply you to me? Why! Hath no other amusing knave got my knack for STAGE BUSINESS?

CONDEL. I said I was—

HEMINGE. Nay. Nor thy Taste—

CONDEL. Even-ness—

HEMINGE. Diverse brilliancies, handsome turns—

CONDEL. Sweet and piercing touches—

HEMINGE. Unac-COUNT-table vocabulary!

CONDEL. —unexpected use of FISHING terms—

HEMINGE. 'Tis YOU we needeth for our desperate hour! Will!

CONDEL. Friend—

HEMINGE. Fellow!

CONDEL. Partner!

HEMINGE. "Shakespeare!"

(Long pause. WILL takes it in, struggling with something in himself.)

WILL. *(Quietly.)* Give the plays to Oxford.

CONDEL. He's not—you.

HEMINGE. Besides. He's got the plague.

WILL. What?

HEMINGE. He lies abandoned at his ancestral home.

CONDEL. Close to death, I've heard. Attended by no one, they say.

HEMINGE. Sorry. Perhaps we should have written.

ANNE. *(Reentering.)* Here's some BEER, and pickled BEETS and some nice—chickweed pie, how long since you've had THAT!

WILL. I have to leave—

ANNE. How funny you are.

(HEMINGE and CONDEL back out.)

CONDEL\HEMINGE. Goodbye, well, Goodbye—wonderful to see you—Will, we'll wait for you at the Inn!

ANNE. What?

WILL. *(To ANNE.)* I'm sorry, but something's come up—

ANNE. Something's come UP! Not one hour ago you swore to me that we were one, all distance forgot, that all would be made well to me—

WILL. I'll write—

(WILL exits)

ANNE. You'll write. YOU'LL WRITE! I can't READ!—you BASTARD!

Scene 10

(Oxford's bedchamber. He is dying. WRIOTHESLEY is with him)

OXFORD. It is too much! I suffer, I burn! A POX upon this PLAGUE!

WRIOTHESLEY. Lie still, you upset yourself and make it worse.

OXFORD. Oh, Henry, curse the fatal infection that doth unknit my bones—I shall die! I shall DIE! Really, you shouldn't be here, Darling— I'm catching.

WRIOTHESLEY. I am here, and here I do remain, until thine end. Where suffering stops, where rest begins. And there are no devouring worms where you will go. They live all above with us the living.

OXFORD. My fever oerwhelms me, quip by quip. I cannot think of anything funny. I cannot think of anything at all. A vacant chamber of aching halls. Oh hell. Who's here?

(WILL enters.)

WRIOTHESLEY. *(Surprised.)* 'Tis Will—.

OXFORD. I hear my Muse hath fled me for a Country Dwelling.

WILL. My Lord, my noble friend—

OXFORD. Do you weep, sensitive Will, Gentle Will, Usurping WILL, Who has won thy bread, and made thy bed in borrowed fame? Who dare to couple with the Great under cover of thy NAME?

WRIOTHESLEY. Hush, Edward! Why do you abuse him that loves you? Mark how his tears do flow for you—

OXFORD. Dying makes one out of temper, Will. Forgive your friend, and think not ill of me when I am gone.

(WILL moves to him, sinks down next to bed.)

WILL. My Lord—whose friendship gave me everything.

OXFORD. I said that in we two hath Nature's Genius met Art's. But I could not have thought of FALSTAFF!

(He begins choking.)

WRIOTHESLEY. This railing doth further thy infirmity.

OXFORD. Long live thee in thy clarity, friend. And by the way, that was no whore, that was thy wife.

WRIOTHESLEY. Why do you tell him that?

WILL. *(Looking up.)* What is that thou tell'st me?

OXFORD. That darksome, gamesome toothsome bawd that we two did board was thy wife pretending to thee for love's sake—she was thine own!

WILL. Ahh! Wilt thou destroy the purity of my WIFE and the attraction of my MISTRESS in ONE FOUL REVELATION?

WRIOTHESLEY. Shame, Edward.

WILL. Cuckold me AGAIN, this last upon thy death bed—who cannot even lift thy diseased fig for a CHOIRBOY?!

WRIOTHESLEY.

—Even upon thy end to twist thy knife—

So foul, so needless, and so cruel a sport?

OXFORD. I know, I know, but it remembereth me what it was to be ALIVE! Remember this, sweet Will. She loved thee well— BEFORE SHE WENT TO BED WITH ME!

(He starts laughing, which starts him coughing.)

WILL. Godspeed. I shall miss your wit and learning, but not your Lordship's cruel humours.

OXFORD. Wait. Will, I had a play I never dared to show.

(He rises unsteadily and crosses to his trunk of manuscripts, d.s. near his writing table. Kneels by it.)

WILL. Why tellst thou me now? When thou hast kick't me shall I love this news or give a damn?

OXFORD. *(Retrieves an old play script. He handles it tenderly.)* About a man who loves a man and dare not show it. Take it for me, finish it—and proclaim me when I am dead. It's called *Twelfth Night*, in which a boy loves a lord. And almost dies of it.

WILL. *(Uncomfortable.)* Why look you meaningfully upon me?

OXFORD. *(Looks away.)* Unlike my life unlucky, it has a pleasing end where love triumphs. It was something like my story as a boy, and I wish it were told.

(OXFORD starts back to his bed.)

WILL. Why should I do it?

OXFORD. *(With some remaining flourish.)* Because as true as 'tis thou hast great gift for poetry, its also true thou hast no gift for plot. And this *Twelfth Night* has a good plot. *(Gives WILL manuscript.)* But call it—*(Weakening.)*—what you will. *(WRIOTHESELEY helps him to bed.)* That which I fed on, consumest me!!

(OXFORD's eyes close.)

WRIOTHESLEY. So far does his disease progress, he stealeth Marlowe's motto. Take him not bitterly, sweet Will. Thy tears wet his hand—that could not shed a tear himself. Thy WORKS shall be when we shall be forgot. Take his trunk of manuscripts, make them live as he could not.

(WILL crosses to trunk. OXFORD gestures for him to take it. He does. Crosses out of Oxford's chambers, starts up the stairs to the above. He turns out, and from behind him, the figure of GEOFFREY enters—a dream-image of the boy-player that sang in Stratford so many years ago. He stands above.)

GEOFFREY. *(Singing, simple and sweet.)*
And so in the mind of man, below as so above
Everything from nothing comes—
To those who—love—.

(GEOFFREY looks toward SHAKESPEARE, SHAKESPEARE looks towards us.
Lights fade.)

END OF PLAY

NOTES for the staging of *THE TAMING OF THE SHREW*
(beginning on page 73)

This scene has certain shape requirements. In order for it to play coherently, it needs to be very specifically scored and detailed. Whatever choices are made in terms of movement, sound, and choreography, they must allow Elizabeth to be the reactive focal point of the scene. She is the organizing element of the hyperactive play beneath—so either by stop-actions, occasional slow-motions, or accidentally placed "gaps" the audience needs to know to look to her for her key moments.

What follows is the essential "story board" of "Shrew's" plot-points to be used for the play within the play. Generally, the strategy might be to tell the story of the Shrew like an old-fashioned silent movie, a musical score providing bursts of ten seconds or so of Renaissance-style Chase Music, as the players scramble to form themselves into an image from Shakespeare's play. The music\tableau needs to hold briefly, so that Elizabeth can interject, then the company has another ten seconds of frenetic or acrobatic physical transition, exaggerated character walk, etc. to form into the next tableau. An attractive solution is to use a drop that they constantly rotate around, emerging into different scene-moments, so the movement flow is constant. Elizabeth's interjections have been written to comment on the following moments from Shakespeare's *Taming of the Shrew*. All of the players can be used for all the images.

From page 75, picking up after

ELIZABETH. What doth the idiot? He hath not another line there! He doth overspeak his part!

OXFORD. What sayeth her Magna Regina?
ELIZABETH. Nay, I spoke of nothing. Hush! Petruchio is to TAKE her now. You shall see!

(Music. Action. Tableau—PETRUCHIO joining KATE in a forced embrace before an exaggeratedly astonished BAPTISTA.)

ELIZABETH. *(Aroused.)* NOW she shall come to know her keeper's call!

(Music. Action. Tableau—Two SUITORS, one with a broken lute over his head, Tableau—KATE melodramatically weeping, stood up at her wedding—before sniggering BIANCA, unhappy BAPTISTA, and perturbed GUESTS. PETRUCHIO and GRUMIO lurk.)

ELIZABETH. *(Deeply moved.)* Left alone at the altar, oh poor girl!

(Music. Action. Tableau—PETRUCHIO abducting KATE on his back as COMPANY mimes chase. GRUMIO holding them at bay.)

ELIZABETH. *(Enthralled.)* SEE how he snatches her away from all the guests!

(Music. Action. Tableau—The taunting starvation of KATE by GRUMIO—as hidden PETRUCHIO and "SERVANTS" watch.)

ELIZABETH. *(Thrilled.)* Cut down to SIZE! How like you THAT, my Girl!

(Music. Action. Tableau—KATE and PETRUCHIO join hands, a happy procession behind them.)

ELIZABETH. *(Ecstatic.)* Ay me! What a story! How will it end!

(There is a little trill of happy resolve music. COMPANY restores to real time.)

PETRUCHIO. Lord how bright and goodly shines the moon! *(And etc.)*

PROPS / *ACT I*

Scene 1: Old Barn in Stratford
Hay bale
Remote controlled rat
Water bucket

Scene 2: Stratford Guild Hall
8 x 5 platform with block
Pedestal
Hay bale
Conquest of Alexandrio curtain on
     poles
Little bird (for finger)
2 Lutes
Finger cymbals
Wicker basket
Porridge pot
Serving spoon
5 Bowls
5 Spoons
4 Stools
Sack
6 Bottles of ale
Small bundle for Geoffrey
Bundle on stick (Will)

Scene 3:London—Backstage of Theatre
8 x 5 platform with landing unit
5 Galatea sides in folder
2 Severed heads
Broom

Condel's chair
Mop
2 Lutes

Scene 4: Ancient Manor— Bedchamber of Edward De Vere, Earl of Oxford
Divan
Bed sheet with Oxford's crest
Taper candle in holder (electric)
Primitive curling iron
Trunk with dressing
Desk with dressing
Quill and inkwell
Hourglass
Books
Papers (pages of *Titus Andronicus*)
Manuscripts
Skull
Poem: *Beautiful Boy*
Possible desk dressing:
     Gyroscope
     Thumbscrew
     Crystals
     Specimens
Rook (bird on wire)
Campaign chair
Refuse/debris
Lute for Minstrel
Wine bottles

Scene 5: Rehearsal

8 x 5 platform with landing unit
    and step unit
Divan (on platform)
Spear
2 *Cleopatra, Queen of the Nilus*
    manuscripts (Fitch, Condel,
    Heminge)
Stool
Oxford's *Titus Andronicus*
    manuscript, rolled and tied
2 Shillings
Food—bread
Dagger

Scene 6: The Court

5 *Venus and Adonis* manuscripts
    (small books)
5 Caption placards for courtiers
6 x 3 platform
Throne
Queen's Riding Crop

Scene 7: Oxford's Rooms

Single *Venus and Adonis*
    manuscript (small book)
Stack of new *Venus and Adonis*
    books, tied
Desk with dressing
Books and papers
Hourglass
Quill and inkwell
Art of English Poesy book

Rape of Lucrece manuscript
Campaign chair

Scene 8: Barn in Stratford

Letter with 10 shillings in pouch
Bowl of milk

Scene 9: The Theatre

8 x 5 platform with landing unit
    and step unit
Condel's chair
2 Stools
Spear
Powder horn
Books
Sewing kit with material
Elizabethan crossword
Barrel (makeshift table)
Loose *Titus Andronicus*
    manuscript pages, some
    blank (large stack)
Quill and inkwell
Bloody tongue
Bloody arm stumps, squirting
Liquid stage blood
Bag of weapons, including swords
    and scabbards
Water jug
Cup

PROPS / *ACT II*

Scene 1: London—Will's Room

8 x 5 platform with bedding and
    bedposts
Will's desk with dressing
Quill and inkwell
5-8 Books
Wine bottle
4 Wine goblets
Whip/riding crop
Makeshift bondage straps
    (hanging from bedpost)
Blank book
Menaechmi of Plautus manu-
    script, rolled and tied
Bag with Lucy's stuff
Tray with Lucy's stuff

Scene 2: Oxford's Room

Sheet with Oxford's crest

Scene 3: Shakspere's Room

Will's desk with dressing
Quill and inkwell
Paper
Poem: *"Two loves have I, one of
    comfort and one of false hair ..."*
Mirror

Scene 4: Road to Stratford

Stratford/London road sign on
    rolling stand

Scene 5: The Court

2 Copies of *Shakespeare's Sonnets*
6 x 3 platform with throne dressing
Walking stick
Bandage for Geoffrey

Scene 6: The Theatre

8 x 5 platform with landing unit
2 additional step units or blocks
Taming of a Shrew manuscript
Cane
Slapstick
Stool
Tankard of ale
Inflatable club
2 Wood blocks
Taming of a Shrew prompt script
Broken lute
Bouquet of flowers
Hourglass
2 Riding horses (stick ponies)
Sack of money
Fan
Plastic water cup
2 Baskets of rose petals
Empty tin plate
Plate with attached food and loose
    leg of mutton
Sun on pole
"Costumed" dummy
Bacon's large, thick manuscript

Derby's manuscript, rolled and tied
Walshingham's manuscript, rolled and tied
Lettice's manuscript, rolled and tied
Lord of Essex's manuscript, rolled and tied
Florio's manuscript, rolled and tied
Bucket/basket
Stuffed greyhound on leash and wheels
Walking stick

Scene 8: Heath Near Stratford

8 x 5 platform with landing unit and 2 step units
Wine bottle
Road sign for heath, on stationary stand

Scene 9: The Barn

Hay bale
Stool
Bundle of wool
2 Wool carders
4 Tankards of ale
Tray with pickled beets and chickweed pie

Scene 10: Oxford's Castle

Divan
2 Pillows

Oxford's sheet
Trunk filled with rolled and tied Manuscripts
Low brazier (incense burner)
Spit bucket
Bloody rags
Twelfth Night manuscript

Gallery Dressing

Stuffed bear
Asses head
Trunks
Severed heads and hands
Staggs/pikes in Stanton
Stuffed boar
Loose straw

GOOD BOYS
Jane Martin

A fierce encounter between fathers, one black and one white, opens a deeply disturbing chapter in their lives. The men relive the school shooting in which their sons died, one a victim and the other the shooter. When racial issues threaten to derail all hope for understanding and forgiveness, the black father's other son pushes the confrontation to a dangerous and frightening climax. This topical drama by the author of *Keely and Du* and other contemporary hits premiered at the Guthrie Theater. "Galvanizing."—*St. Paul Pioneer*. "A terrifying, terrific piece of theatre that is as memorable as it is unsettling."—*Star Tribune*. (#9935)

THE ANASTASIA TRIALS
IN THE COURT OF WOMEN
Carolyn Gage

This farcical play-within-a-play is an excursion into a world of survivors and abusers. It opens as a feminist theatre group is about to put sisterhood to an iron test: each draws the role she will play on this evening from a hat. The performance that follows is the conspiracy trial of five women accused of denying Anastasia Romanov her identity. The audience votes to over-rule or sustain each motion, creating a different play at every performance. "Farce, social history, debate play, agitprop, audience-participation melodrama, satire [that] makes the head reel!"—*San Diego Union-Tribune*. Wild."—*Washington Blade*. 9 f. (#3742)

Send for your copy of the Samuel French
BASIC CATALOGUE OF PLAYS AND MUSICALS

JUMP / CUT
Neena Beber

Winner of the L. Arnold Weissberger Award

Three bright urbanites want to make their mark on the world. Paul is a hardworking film-maker on the rise. His girlfriend Karen, a grad student, must get on with her thesis or find a life outside of academia. Dave, a life-long buddy whose brilliance is being consumed by increasingly severe episodes of manic-depression, is camping on Paul's couch. Paul and Karen decide to turn Paul into a documentary. The camera is on 24 hours a day, capturing up-close images of his jags and torpors and their responses. How far will love, friendship and ambition take this hip trio? "A remarkable, absorbing, complex and intelligent play."—*Variety*. 2 m., 1 f. (#12918)

STRANGER
Craig Lucas

Strangers on a transcontinental flight gradually reveal things they have never spoken about before: Linda is traveling with a great deal of cash as well as enough pills to kill herself; Hush has just been released from prison after serving fifteen years for kidnapping a young girl and keeping her alive inside a trunk for over a year. An alliance grows based on the shocking aspects of their personal histories. Together they go to a crude cabin in the middle of nowhere where they learn things about themselves and each other that change their lives irrevocably. A mystery, a tragedy, a love story, a requiem and a jaw-dropping shocker, *Stranger* is not suitable for bedtime reading. 2 m., 2 f. (#21446)

Send for your copy of the Samuel French
BASIC CATALOGUE OF PLAYS AND MUSICALS